THE MYTH BUSTER

150 Great Misconceptions Clarified

THE MYTH BUSTER

150 Great Misconceptions Clarified

Dr N. C. Asthana, IPS

M.Sc., Ph.D.

&

Dr Anjali Nirmal

M.A., Ph.D.

STERLING PAPERBACKS
An imprint of
Sterling Publishers (P) Ltd.
A-59, Okhla Industrial Area, Phase-II,
New Delhi-110020.
Tel: 26387070, 26386209; Fax: 91-11-26383788
E-mail: sterlingpublishers@airtelmail.in
ghai@nde.vsnl.net.in
www.sterlingpublishers.com

The Myth Buster: 150 Great Misconceptions Clarified

ISBN 978- 81-207-4210-9

Printed and Published by Sterling Publishers Pvt. Ltd.,
New Delhi-110 020.

Preface

One thing that we lack very seriously in India is rational and scientific temper. Even the educated people of India do not have a rational temperament. We are too willing to accept most things as the ultimate truth simply because some third-rate reporter wrote about them in the local paper or some TV channel had shown it. It has nothing to do with our religiosity. That people abandon logic when it comes to matters religious can be easily understood; what is most disappointing is that they are culturally and socially attuned to believe in everything that has been handed down to them by what they heard in childhood, what their parents or relatives told them, what they read in magazines, what they saw in the advertisements or in some serial on TV. If people believed in the claim of the idols of Lord Ganesha drinking milk, it can be understood as a result of religious fervour; however, if they believe that there would be a miscarriage if a pregnant woman happens to eat a piece of papaya then it shows nothing but the great general ignorance which pervades all walks of life.

This is the very first book of its kind in the world that covers a wide range of subjects ranging from beauty, fashion, lifestyle, health, exercise, sex, diet, nutrition, general science, astrology, medicine, sports, miracles, and supernatural phenomena to terrorism. In these pages, you will find the most authentic information on all these topics citing internationally renowned authorities, which will literally lead you to the truth.

Indians do not have the habit of questioning beliefs of any kind. There are numerous myths in every walk of life which even people with Science background nurture all their lives. The purpose of writing this book is to dispel various myths, which people harbour and thereby educate them and make them more rational. No science education is necessary to understand and enjoy this book. The topics are written in an interesting and informative style.

Dr N. C. Asthana, IPS
Dr Anjali Nirmal

Contents

Preface v

Part I

BEAUTY, FASHION AND LIFESTYLE

1. Can Fairness Creams Really Make You Fairer? 3
2. Can You Get Rid Of Dandruff By Home Remedies? 5
3. Does Eating Chocolate Or Fried Food Leads To More Pimples? 7
4. Would A Woman Get Thicker Hair If She Shaved Her Legs Or Arms? 9
5. Can Costly Or Imported Cosmetics Make You Look Young? 11
6. Can You Get Long, Luxurious Hair By Using Hair Oils? .. 13
7. Can Your Skin Be Rejuvenated By Facials And Are They Safe? 15
8. Are Herbal Cosmetics Any Better Or Safer Than Regular Cosmetics? 17
9. Are Sunscreens As Effective As They Claim? 19
10. Do Costly Or Imported Skin Care Cosmetics Really Work Wonders? 21
11. Does Using The AXE Deodorant Make A Man Attractive To Women? 23
12. All The Mysterious Treatments That You Get At Luxury Spas: Do They Really Work? 25
13. Is It Really Safe And Worthwhile To Take Botox Treatment For Removing Wrinkles? 27
14. Can You Get Rid Of Cellulite By Anti-Cellulite Creams? .. 29

Part II

HEALTH AND EXERCISE

15. Can You Get a Flat Abdomen By Doing Sit-Ups Or Abdominal Exercises Alone? 33

16. Can Your Height Increase By Wearing Acupressure Sandals? 35
17. Can Eating Sweets Lead To Diabetes? 37
18. Does A Woman Become Muscle-Bound If She Practices Weight Training? 39
19. Can Wearing Rudraksha Reduce Blood Pressure? 41
20. Can Wearing Magnetic Wristbands Help In Relieving Pain Of Arthritis And Other Ailments? 43
21. Are The New Age Exercise Fads Any Beneficial? 45
22. Are Antibacterial Soaps Any Better Than Plain Soaps? 47
23. Does Reiki Really Have Any Miraculous Health Benefits? 49
24. Can You Really Get Any Health Benefit By Pranic Healing? 51
25. Can Smoking Low-Nicotine Cigarettes Help In Reducing Chances Of Cancer? 53
26. Can Taking Large Doses Of Vitamin C Help In Preventing Common Cold? 55
27. Can Calcium In Toothpaste Make Your Teeth Stronger And Help Fight Germs For 12 Hours? 57
28. Is The Morning Walker Machine Of Any Use? 59
29. How Effective Are Pain Relief Creams? 61
30. Can Reading In Poor Light Affect Your Eyesight And Other Myths Related To Vision? 63
31. Are Sauna Baths Beneficial? 65
32. Does Red Wine Have Any Great Medicinal Value? 67
33. Is There Any Significance Of The So-Called Cooling Crystals In Toothpaste? 69
34. Is The So-Called Detoxification Of The Body Really Possible? 71

Part III

DIET AND NUTRITION

35. Can 'An Apple A Day Really Keep The Doctor Away'? 75
36. Can You Lose Weight By Drinking Honey And Lemon In Warm Water? 77

37. Can Taking Muesli In Breakfast Make You Highly Energetic? ... 79
38. Is Spinach Really A Good Source Of Iron As It Is Believed To Be? ... 81
39. Do New Age Diet Fads Really Work? ... 83
40. Is Eating Walnuts Or Almonds Good For The Brain? ... 85
41. Is There Anything Particularly Good About The So-Called Probiotic Ice Cream? ... 87
42. Is The Costly Green Tea Any Better Than The Ordinary Black Tea? ... 89
43. Are Fancy Energy Drinks Like Red Bull Of Any Value At All? ... 91
44. Is Genetically Modified (GM) Food Perfectly Safe To Eat? ... 93
45. Are Soya Protein And Tofu Really As Good As They Are Believed To Be? ... 95
46. Will Eating Cornflakes Improve Your Brainpower? ... 97
47. Is Drinking Tea Without Milk Any Better Than Drinking Tea With Milk? ... 99
48. Is Organic Food Any Better Than Ordinary Food? ... 101
49. Is There Any Nutritive Value In Coca-Cola And Other Soft Drinks? ... 103
50. Are Antioxidants Really Miraculous Health Supplements? ... 105
51. Can Certain Food Items Lower Cholesterol Level? ... 107

Part IV

SEX

52. Is Masturbation Harmful In Any Way? ... 111
53. Is There Any Particular Food Or Drink That Can Work As Aphrodisiac Or Increase Your Sexual Desire? ... 113
54. Can Drinking Milk On The Wedding Night Help You In Any way? ... 115
55. Does Size Matter? ... 117
56. Is It Possible To Increase The Length And Girth Of Penis By Medicines And Exercise? ... 119

57. Does Breast Size Have Anything To Do With The Sexuality Or Feminineness Of A Woman? 121
58. Can The Size Of Breasts Be Increased By Applying Creams, Massage Or Exercise? 123
59. Can Anyone Take Viagra And Is It Safe? 125
60. Does Observing Celibacy Make One Stronger And Should Wrestlers Be Celibate? 127
61. Is Indulging In Excessive Sex Harmful? 129
62. Does Sex In Old Age Do Any Harm? 131

Part V

MIRACLES, SUPERNATURAL PHENOMENA AND STUNTS

63. Can Some People Bend Spoons Or Move Objects By Mental Power? 135
64. Is Telepathy Possible? 137
65. Is There Anything Real About Black Magic? 139
66. Can Some Sadhus Or Stuntmen Lie On A Bed Of Nails? 141
67. How Do Miracle Workers Get A Heavy Stone Broken On Their Chests? 143
68. Can Some Yogis Bury Themselves In Pits For Several Days? 145
69. Do Ghosts Really Exist? 147
70. Is There Anything Really Mysterious At The Bermuda Triangle? 149
71. How Can Some People Walk On Broken Glass? 151
72. Can Some Strong Men Really Hold Several Cars By Their Arms? 153
73. Do Pyramids Possess Miraculous Powers? 155
74. How Do Some People Manage To Walk On Burning Coals? 157
75. How Do Fire-Breathers Show Their Stunts? 159
76. What Is Psychic Surgery And Can Miracle Workers Really Operate On A Person With Bare Hands? 161

77. What Is Faith Healing And Can It Really Work? 163
78. What Is Exorcism And Can People Be Really 'Possessed' By Ghosts? 165
79. Is There Any Basis To Numerology? 167
80. Do Vampires Really Exist? 169
81. Can Black Magic Or Some Other Trick Bring Back The Dead And Make Them Zombies? 171
82. What Are Séances Or Planchettes And Can You Talk To The Spirits Through Such Things? 173
83. How Do Some Religiously Devout People Burn Camphor On Their Hands Or Tongues? 175
84. How Do Some People Swallow Swords? 177
85. Can Some People Really Chew Glass And Swallow It? 179
86. Do Some Animals Have A Sixth Sense By Which They Can Predict Death? 181
87. Are The So-Called Out-Of-Body Experiences (OBE) Claimed By Some People Real? 183
88. Is There Really Anything Called ESP (Extra-Sensory Perception)? 185

Part VI

GENERAL SCIENCE

89. Can Mobile Phones Cause Cancer? 189
90. Does Alternating Current Pull You Towards The Source? . 191
91. Is A Detergent Powder That Produces More Foam Better Than A Detergent Which Produces Less Foam? 193
92. Does Cigarette Smoking Help In Concentration? 195
93. Does Drinking Alcohol Or Eating Chicken Help You Cope Better With Cold Weather? 197
94. Does A Large Head Or Large Forehead Mean That The Person Would Be More Intelligent? 199
95. Can Hypnotists Really Take Complete Control Of Your Mind? 201
96. Are The So-Called Acupressure Seats In Cars Of Any Use At All? 203

97. Is Time Travel Possible: Can One Visit The Past Or The Future? 205
98. Do Flying Saucers Or UFOs Really Come To The Earth? 207
99. Is Yawning Contagious? 209
100. What Should You Do When Lightning Is Striking: Will You Be Safe Inside A Car? 211
101. Can The Ray Guns Of Star Wars Be Made For Real? 213
102. Is There An X-Ray Or Some Other Imaging System That Can See Through Your Clothes? 215
103. Are You More Likely To Be Struck By Lightning If You Use A Mobile Phone During A Thunderstorm? 217
104. Is It Possible To Travel To The Stars? 219
105. Will An Aircraft Rupture And Fall Due To Pressurised Cabins If A Bullet Is Shot Through It From Inside? 221
106. Is There Any Good Reason For Mobile Phones To Be Not Used On Aircrafts? 223
107. Does A Bull Get Really Enraged On Seeing A Piece Of Red Cloth? 225
108. Is It Possible To Deceive A Breath Alcohol Analyser? 227
109. Will A Microwave Oven Explode If You Accidentally Place Some Metal In It? 229
110. Can Sharks Smell Human Blood From A Great Distance? 231
111. Are The Fears Of Global Warming Justified? 233
112. Does CNG Really Cause Lesser Pollution Than Diesel? 235
113. Can Our Energy Problems Be Solved By Solar Power? 237

Part VII

ASTROLOGY

114. Can Tarot Cards Tell Your Future And Help You Solve Your Problems? 241
115. Can Feng Shui Be Of Any Help In Your Life? 243
116. Can Crystal Ball Gazers Tell Your Future? 245

Part VIII

MEDICINE

117. If A Pregnant Woman Eats Papaya, Will It Lead To Miscarriage? 249
118. Can Hair Oil Reduce Mental Tension? 251
119. Is A Chyawanprash Containing Gold And Silver Any Better Than Ordinary Chyawanprash? 253
120. Are Cough Drops And Cough Mixtures Of Any Real Therapeutic Value? 255
121. Does Laughter Therapy Have Any Use? 257
122. Is Taking Antibiotics In Viral Fevers Of Any Help At All? 259
123. Can You Catch A Cold By Going Out In Cold Weather? 261
124. Can You Get Leucoderma If You Eat Fish And Milk Together? 263
125. Does Massage Have Any Therapeutic Value At All? 265
126. Are Angioplasty And Stents As Useful As They Are Claimed To Be? 267
127. Is It Hygienic To Pick Up And Eat A Dropped Food Item Within Five Seconds? 269
128. Do Popular Hangover Remedies Really Work? 271
129. Is Aromatherapy Of Any Use At All? 273
130. Is Watching TV Safe For Kids Below Three Years Of Age? 275

Part IX

SPORTS AND MARTIAL ARTS

131. Is There Anything Mysterious About The Breaking Of Tiles, Boards And Slabs By Karate Practitioners? 279
132. Do Martial Artists Possess Any Mysterious Energy Called 'Chi'? 281
133. Is There Any Significance Of The Loud Shout Of The Martial Artists When They Punch Or Kick? 283
134. The Famous Skull Mark Made By The Punch Of Phantom – Can It Be Ever Made In Real Life? 285

135. Are The Violent Throws And Strikes Made In Pro-Wrestling Real? 287

Part X
TERRORISM

136. Can Terrorists Make LPG Or Petrol Tankers Explode Like Bombs By Shooting At Them? 291
137. After Every Blast The Media Says That RDX Was Used: How Credible Are The Claims? 293
138. Can Terrorists Really Blow Up Dams? 295
139. Can Terrorists Really Unleash Biological Warfare On Huge Populations? 297
140. Can Terrorists Resort To Chemical Warfare Or Use Chemical Agents In Their Attacks? 299
141. Can Terrorists Make And Use The So-Called 'Dirty Nuclear Bombs'? 301

Part XI
MYTHS PROPAGATED BY FILMS

142. Will The Earth Be Destroyed If It Is Hit By An Asteroid Or Comet? 305
143. Can We Save The Earth From An Asteroid Hurtling Towards Us By Blowing It Up Using A Hydrogen Bomb? 307
144. Do Grenades Produce A Ball Of Fire When They Explode And Can They Throw Men Around? 309
145. Can Locks Be Broken By Shooting At Them With Pistols Or Revolvers? 311
146. Do Cars Really Fly Up In The Air If The Fuel Tank Explodes Or When They Run Over A Landmine? 313
147. How Do People Jump Through Glasses In Films? 315
148. How Do They Show A Burning Man In Films? 317
149. Does A Man Hit By A Bullet Fall Backwards? 319
150. Gunshots And Gunshot Wounds: How Are They Made In Films? 321

Part I

BEAUTY, FASHION AND LIFESTYLE

1

Can Fairness Creams Really Make You Fairer?

To the average Indian man and woman 'fair is beautiful'. You only have to look at the matrimonial advertisements in any newspaper and you will understand this instantly. A girl with a typically Indian complexion seems to have no chance! This has led to a great market of fairness creams, which lure women in various ways. A dark-complexioned girl is shown sulking whereas once she makes up her mind to use the fairness cream, she either lands with a good husband in a few weeks or a glamorous job like that of a model. But do they really work, or more correctly, can they really work? The answer is a categorical no. It is only clever and unethical advertising. They are only selling a dream. They have never produced a single girl who became even a shade fairer by using these creams.

Scientific research disproves their claims entirely. The colour of the skin depends on the amount of the pigment melanin that is produced by the cells called melanocytes. This is an internal process. There is no way an external application of something can stop or reverse this internal process or change the basic skin tone that you have inherited. Scientists have analysed and found that most of the fairness creams sold in India contain either chemicals like titanium dioxide or niacinamide or hydrolysed milk proteins. Titanium dioxide can only protect from ultraviolet rays and thus prevent sunburn. Creams sold as ayurvedic preparations generally contain extracts of roses, aloe vera, walnuts, oranges, saffron, licorice, wheat germs and even pearls. There is no scientific evidence that they can lighten the colour of the skin by reducing the amount of melanin in it. On the contrary, they can cause damage at the cellular level like sloughing.

Elsewhere in the world, chemicals like hydroquinone have been tried which inhibit the synthesis of melanin. Thus it can counter the effect of excessive pigment produced as a result of exposure to sun. But they have serious side effects and you may well end up looking like Michael Jackson.

2

Can You Get Rid of Dandruff By Home Remedies?

Dandruff is a universal problem. You can look up in any fashion or lifestyle magazine and half of the queries would be about dandruff. There is no end to the advice you get from laymen on how to get rid of dandruff. The remedies used range from lime juice, green gram powder, beetroots, snake gourd, yoghurt that has been kept in the open for three days, and fenugreek to a concoction of hair oils. The fact is that none of them work. Had they been working, there would not have been such a large number of people suffering from it.

Most people do not know that dandruff is caused by many different reasons. Hence a single remedy cannot work against all types of dandruff even if it is a medication. One of the most common causes of dandruff is the fungus Malassezia globosa (previously called P. Ovale). This fungus is treated only by specific antifungal preparations like ketoconazole. Shampoos containing ketoconazole are easily available. Nothing else would help this dandruff. In some people, excessive secretion of the sebaceous gland causes dandruff. Shampooing daily helps such cases. On the other hand excessive shampooing, particularly with harsh ones, could actually increase the dandruff in some people. Some shampoos are sold with sulphur or salicylic acid in them. All that they do is loosen the flakes so that they may be washed away easily, but they do not treat dandruff. In some cases, dandruff is the result of seborrheic dermatitis. They are helped by shampoos containing zinc pyrithione or selenium sulphide. The New York University Medical Center has found that shampoos reduce the rate at which the scalp cells multiply and thus reduce the production of dandruff. Some cases of dandruff are caused by excessive dryness in the scalp. They respond to application of oil and mild shampooing. In some cases allergy occurs due to certain hair gels or sprays. The only way is to stop using the product.

Thus you can see that no home remedy for dandruff can work.

3

Does Eating Chocolate or Fried Food Leads To More Pimples?

Acne or pimples are a matter of great concern to youngsters. Many people continue to get them even late in life. Half the questions in magazines deal with pimples. It is generally said that eating chocolate or fried food leads to more acne. Is it really so?

When the hair follicles (or pores) get blocked for some reason, the sebum (oil) too gets blocked. If it remains like that for some time, then you get blackheads or whiteheads. If bacteria grow in them then you get pimples. Why it all happens is a very complex process. In adolescents it is due to hormonal reasons. Other reasons include excessive secretion of sebaceous glands, use of anabolic steroids, exposure to chlorine compounds, pregnancy and polycystic ovary syndrome, etc.

There is not the slightest evidence that eating chocolate or fried food leads to or aggravates acne. Eating excessive fried food or high calorie food like chocolates may make you fatter but there is no reason that it will make your sebaceous glands hyperactive or block the pores. Had it been true, every fat person should have been suffering from pimples, but it is not so. In fact it is not at all necessary that fat persons should also have oily skins. For that matter, every person with oily skin does not get pimples.

Many other myths surround pimples – which it is caused by stress, masturbation, or poor hygiene. Generally people think that blackheads are caused by dirt. But it is not so. Dirt does not block the hair follicle. The blockage occurs when the walls of the pores stick together. Frequent washing of the face does not help this. Most of the creams that are sold for removing pimples contain a simple substance called benzoyl peroxide. This may kill the bacteria on the surface but will not prevent the blockages or infections from occurring again. Drugs like isotrenitoin can reduce oil secretion but only for some time. For proper treatment you may require antibiotic creams containing erythromycin or clindamycin and oral antibiotics like tetracycline or doxycycline.

4

Would A Woman Get Thicker Hair If She Shaved Her Legs Or Arms?

A lot of women are plagued by the problem of body hair, particularly on the legs and arms. There is a very popular belief, augmented by advertisements of hair-removing products, that shaving is for men and if a woman shaves she will get more and thicker hair. This is not true. The companies have propagated this myth because shaving is a much cheaper option and if women resort to shaving, the sales of their creams would suffer.

The extent of body hair depends on the hormonal balance in the body. A boy of 10 years does not have a beard because the male hormones in his body have not yet reached the level for a beard to grow. He will not grow a beard merely by shaving. Men of some races like the Chinese and Japanese have very little facial hair – do they get extra hair merely by shaving every day? Shaving is a purely mechanical action. There is no way it can or should result in excessive growth of hair or make hair thicker.

The only side effect of shaving is that there may be cuts if it is not done carefully. For that matter, waxing with hot wax is very painful and waxing with cold wax is also considerably painful. Depilatory creams may irritate sensitive skin, particularly in the armpits and the pubic region. In comparison, shaving is painless and reaction-free. Electric razors and costly electric epilators basically serve the same function as shaving – they too remove the hair – but are not criticised as they are costly whereas shaving is cheaper. For waxing one may have to go to a beauty parlour and spend much more. That shaving has to be done more often is a different thing, but there is no reason to believe that a waxed leg is more silky or smooth than a shaved leg. A shaved leg that is properly moisturised and creamed is equally smooth.

5

Can Costly Or Imported Cosmetics Make You Look Young?

Cosmetics are a multi-billion dollar industry. They thrive on the eternal desire of women to look young forever. A host of cosmetics are sold that claim to give you a younger looking skin. Can they do so? What is the truth? The costliest of them claim to have effective chemicals like peptides, antioxidants, ceramides and idebenones in them. Scientists have found that they cannot work. You see, for a chemical to work inside the skin, it must undergo a desired chemical reaction within the inner parts of the skin. But this is not possible. In the first place, cosmetics cannot penetrate the skin. Secondly, the Journal of Investigative Dermatology also reports that, even if they do, they are broken down by the enzymes present in the skin and become ineffective.

There is nothing miraculous about these chemicals. Peptides are small portions of proteins. Any chemical that decreases the rate of oxidation is called antioxidant or more accurately a reducing agent. In the cosmetic industry they call it free-radical damage to the skin to confuse the consumer. Idebenones are antioxidants. Ceramides are skin fats. Now if the skin has aged or wrinkled, it is the result of complex internal processes. There are complex chemical changes inside the body – some chemicals are produced more, some less. The overall effect shows up on the skin also. There is no research to prove that applying such chemicals externally will fight what is happening inside. The extent of wrinkling depends on your diet, heredity, skin type, amount of sleep, etc. As Paula Begoun, author of *Don't Go to the Cosmetics Counter Without Me* points out, if the skin has lost its support structure or collagen, making it less elastic, how can a cream replenish it from inside the skin? Even if the damage is caused due to external factors such as working for long hours in the sun, the damage still remains internal. An external application, whether herbal or non-herbal, cannot undo what has happened internally.

6

Can You Get Long, Luxurious Hair By Using Hair Oils?

The market is flooded with a large number of hair oils. Some of them add few Indian herbs and fruits like *amla* to them. All the hair oils sold in India try to blind the consumer in the name of tradition. Some proclaim themselves to be of ayurvedic formulations. All these are absolutely false. The fact is that Charak and Sushruta were not bothered with hair care and beauty as we understand them today – they were concerned with holistic health and internal medicine. Others merely cite the authority of the mythical grandma – she used hair oil and hence her hair was healthy. The fact is that grandma mostly stayed inside the house and was never exposed to sun, heat, dirt, automobile smoke and chemicals in shampoos to which we are exposed every day.

No hair oil, medicated or otherwise, can penetrate the skin and react chemically with the root of the hair to exert any effect. It does not make any difference whether it is coconut, castor, *amla*, *brahmi* or whatever. The scalp is not porous; below the surface of the skin is the hair root, which is enclosed within a hair follicle. At the base of the hair follicle is the dermal papilla. The dermal papilla is fed by the bloodstream, which carries nourishment to produce new hair. There is no way you can give nutrition to the dermal papilla from outside, however exotic the oil may be. Hair growth or loss is an internal process that depends on general health, hormonal balance, genetic factors and even stress.

If the scalp is very dry it may weaken the hair roots. Massaging oil into the scalp may reduce dryness and thus reduce hair fall, but it cannot promote hair growth. Applying oil to the hair serves only one function. It reduces the friction between hairs the way you lubricate your car engine. This reduces hair loss while combing and brushing. The length of the hair, on the other hand, has little to do with the health of the hair. Hair in poor health can also be long.

7

Can Your Skin Be Rejuvenated By Facials And Are They Safe?

The popular belief is that facials done in a beauty parlour or spa is a complete beauty treatment. Many women get it done regularly but those who cannot, see to it that it is done before important occasions. Mostly brides-to-be are very keen on it. Does it really work? Does it really give you a new and rejuvenated skin as they claim? Are you aware of the potential risks and harmful effects?

Facial beauty treatment generally consists of three steps: vigorous massaging of the face with creams, steaming (using a hot towel or a steaming gadget) and application of a face mask containing adsorbents and astringents. Ill-paid and ill-qualified girls using unsterilised equipment and products, which may not suit your skin type at all, generally do facials in beauty parlours.

In a study published in the International Journal of Dermatology by Dr Neena Khanna of AIIMS, a total of 169 instances of women (aged 17-63 years) who had received facial beauty treatment in three well-established beauty parlours in New Delhi, were studied. For massage, the parlours had used standard creams, herbal creams and even exotic creams containing gold salts. Nearly 40% of the women developed puffiness and redness of skin (erythema) as a result of the massage and about one-third of them who got their blackheads removed after steaming developed permanent redness at the site of extraction. At times adverse effects appear after some days. One-third developed dermatitis. In fact in over one-third women, acne eruption increased after the treatment!

Scientists conclude that the benefits of facial are largely psychological. Most women feel better because they think that they have been cared for and that they have got something done for their beauty even if the results are not to be seen in the mirror. Some women feel better because there is a generalised cleansing which they are not able to do on a daily basis and the cream application makes the skin softer whereas some like the relaxation of the massage.

8

Are Herbal Cosmetics Any Better Or Safer Than Regular Cosmetics?

If you have to sell even the most useless thing in India, you must attach the label of herbal on it. You can sell anything under the name 'herbal'. A company in Kerala has started selling a drug called 'Musli Power', and they call it the 'Indian Herbal Viagra'. Pfizer, the manufacturer of Viagra, has filed a case against it. Indians have an inbuilt belief that all things herbal reflect the esoteric knowledge of ayurveda and hence tradition demands that we the Indians must use them. It is easy to mislead the Indians by saying that regular cosmetics have 'chemicals' and they can be harmful. Nobody bothers to question further. For that matter, all herbal products have some kind of chemicals. The entire universe is made up of chemicals only. How could a chemical made in the laboratory be different from the same chemical found in some herb or extracted from the herb? Salt would be sodium chloride only, whether you make it in the laboratory or extract it from the sea water.

The companies selling herbal cosmetics never reveal the chemicals that are active ingredients of the herbal extracts. It is not that they cannot be analysed but the companies deliberately do not examine them because upon analysis it would be found that either there is nothing exotic in the herbal extracts or the identified chemicals do not have the capability of producing the effects they claim.

The flowers and leaves of many plants like rose and chamomile have pleasant smells and they look good too. However, there is not an iota of scientific evidence that they can clear your acne or remove wrinkles. No herbal cosmetic company has ever cited a single research paper published by neutral scientists. And as for their safety claim, the fact remains that many people are allergic to many plant products – in fact the list of herbal products that can cause contact dermatitis is very large. There is no reason to believe that herbal products are necessarily safer.

9

Are Sunscreens As Effective As They Claim?

Earlier Indians never bothered about exposure to the sun. The white races did because they were not used to such bright sun. However, ever since the Indian girls have started becoming Miss Worlds and Miss Universes, they have become very conscious of exposure to the sun. The sun has been maligned as the biggest enemy of complexion. So, the cosmetic industry has taken advantage of this and has flooded the market with a host of sunscreens, which promise to protect your skin from the sun and keep you delicate like a flower. Do they really work?

In moderation, ultraviolet B rays of the sun produce vitamin D, whereas UVA rays penetrate deeper and produces the tanning for which Europeans come to Indian beaches. In excess, both can cause skin damage. Sunscreens have chemicals like PABA (para amino benzoic acid), benzophenone, tinosorb, cinnamate, etc. that absorbs UV rays. Physical sunscreens are materials like zinc oxide and titanium dioxide, which reflects UV rays – this is the white paint that many cricket players use on their lips and cheeks while playing. The Environment Working Group in the USA analysed 783 sunscreen creams and found 84% of them to be absolutely useless even for white skins.

The companies flaunt things like SPF (sun protection factor) only to confuse the consumers. The SPF is nothing but a rating scale to indicate the time required to produce a certain degree of sunburn on protected skin in comparison to that on unprotected skin. A high SPF simply means that a sunscreen-protected skin will take longer to get sunburn. For a sunscreen to work, it should continuously stay on your face. The catch is whether it can stay?

As you move about in the sun or play on the beach, you sweat and this sweat will wash it away. You wipe your face with a handkerchief or tissue and it is gone! You plunge into the pool and it disappears immediately. It will work only if you apply it every 15 minutes – meaning more sales for the company.

10

Do Costly Or Imported Skin Care Cosmetics Really Work Wonders?

All of us have seen the alluring advertisements on TV and in glossy lifestyle magazines that promote very costly imported cosmetics. They boast of chemicals with difficult-sounding names in them and claim to do wonders. It is all clever advertising. Scientists do not support their claims. You see the skin is not a permeable thing. It is not that you could apply just about anything externally and expect it to go inside and do wonders. Had it been so, you would have been soaking a great deal of water while taking a bath in a tub and swelling like a *kishmish* after that. Does it happen? No! You will not soak oil either. Had it been so, bacteria would enter through your skin easily and make you sick every day. Only certain types of molecules can penetrate the skin to some extent. That is how painkiller creams give some relief.

Dr Patricia Engasser, a dermatologist for Kaiser Permanente Medical Center in Redwood City, California says that dry skin, quite like parched earth, becomes less flexible and brittle. Water, glycerin or even petroleum jelly makes it softer, just like water sprayed on parched earth or a shoe polished with wax polish. It is a purely mechanical action and no chemical reaction is involved. The shoe polish does not react with the leather of the shoe. That is all what moisturisers do – they hydrate the skin and add a protective layer to retain the moisture. There is no evidence that chemicals like alpha hydroxy acid (also known as fruit acids in the advertisements for those women who cannot remember the chemical name) have any beneficial effect significantly better than these simple things. It is all hype. In fact it can cause irritation like itching, stinging and burning in sensitive skin. Then the companies add chemicals like natural amino acids to reduce irritation by controlling the release of alpha hydroxy acid. Basically, at first they make a costly but irritating product, then reduce the irritation and claim that it is an improved product even though it remains as ineffective as ever!

11

Does Using The AXE Deodorant Make A Man Attractive To Women?

The AXE deodorant made by the multinational company Unilever shows a rather sexist advertisement on TV in which hordes of scantily-clad women are shown rushing to grab a man on an island who has used it. It is also sold under the brand name Lynx. In their earlier advertisements they used to show women following the man who had used AXE the way rats followed the Pied Piper of Hamelin in the famous fairy tale. Similar advertisements are shown all over the world. In other words, the product claims that its fragrance has some compulsive and biological attraction for women.

Scientists have strongly condemned and refuted this claim. There is no such fragrance in the world that can arouse sexual attraction in women, irrespective of their age or race, and make them compulsively rush towards the human male of any age or race that wears the fragrance. This highly objectionable claim goes against the entire concept of sexual attraction. Incidentally, AXE comes in a number of fragrances and claims that all of them are equally effective. Sexual attraction in animals is largely a biological process. However, sexual attraction in humans is a very complex psychological phenomenon. In animals, there are substances like sex pheromones, which are secreted to indicate that the female is available for breeding. The male animal follows the scent and takes the initiative for courting the female for mating. The nature has not provided a corresponding smell in the male animal for the female animal to pursue the male even when she is in heat! The question of a natural smell in humans does not arise.

There are several scientific reasons as to why it cannot happen with humans. The foremost is that the human female does not periodically come into heat like animals for breeding. Hence the human male does not require a scent to know that. Also the human nose is not as sensitive as the animals'. According to Dr Tristram Wyatt of Oxford University, no pheromonal substance has ever been found to directly influence human behaviour. The claim of AXE is therefore purely mythical.

12

All The Mysterious Treatments That You Get At Luxury Spas: Do They Really Work?

These days the ultimate in luxury consists of spa treatments. Spas do great business, courtesy the rich customers who do not know much about such treatments but are too eager to spend money on every fad. The spas offer a variety of treatments ranging from Watsu, Hot stone therapy, Thalassotherapy, Polarity massage, Vichy shower, Turkish bath, Thai massage, Swiss shower, Shiatsu, Scotch hose and Body wrap, to Paraffin treatment, etc. All these are supposed to relax and rejuvenate you.

Let us see what are these things and can they really work. In Watsu, they rock and stretch your body in water. In Hot stone therapy, they put hot stones at various points on your body and say that it improves circulation. Thalassotherapy uses sea products for exfoliating the skin. Polarity massage is a massage that claims to release energy from your body. A Vichy shower has five to seven showerheads, which pour water onto you while you are lying on a cushioned wet table. The Turkish bath is nothing but a variant of steam bath. In Thai massage, the masseuse may walk on your back, crack knuckles and pull fingers. A Swiss shower consists of powerful shower jets that alternate hot and cold water on various parts of the body; in Scotch hose the same thing is done by the operator. Shiatsu is an acupressure massage. In body wrap you are slathered with a body mask made of algae, seaweed, mud, clay, lotion or cream. In Paraffin treatment, heated paraffin is rubbed all over the body.

There is no evidence that such massages or therapies can cure a medical condition. All that you get in a spa is forced rest; if there is any perceived benefit, it is due to the rest you get from your stressed life. Everybody feels a little better with some pampering. You would feel better even if someone just pressed your feet or forehead. Spas do nothing more – but in a fashionable and very costly way.

13

Is It Really Safe And Worthwhile To Take Botox Treatment For Removing Wrinkles?

These days Botox treatment has acquired the status of the most advanced beauty treatment. It is supposed to remove wrinkles. It has been popularised by MBBS doctors who are not known for any medical knowledge but for moving around in the page-three party circuit with the rich people and acting as consultants for beauty competitions. You must learn the truth that such doctors will never tell you the risks that are associated with Botox treatment because they have made a business out of it.

What is Botox? Botox is a diluted form of a bacterial nerve toxin known as botulinum. This is the toxin that causes botulism or a very dangerous kind of food poisoning. For beauty treatment, small quantities of Botox is injected into the muscles that cause wrinkles when you frown, squint, laugh or smile. These muscles are in the forehead and around the eyes or neck. The toxin paralyses the muscles, as a result they are not able to contract. Since the paralysed muscle lies relaxed, the skin looks smoother. It has become a popular treatment because it takes just about 10 minutes. The results last up to 4 months. To keep the effects, you will need to repeat it every 3 to 6 months.

Ben Kaminsky, a famous dermatological chemist, who has researched on it for 30 years, says that many a times Botox injections can cause harmful side effects. Botox may worsen an existing heart disease or a nerve or muscle disorder such as ALS (Lou Gehrig's disease) or myasthenia gravis. It may cause bruises, stinging or redness around injection sites. Worst, if the quantity injected is slightly miscalculated you may not be able to raise your eyelids or your lips may be paralysed as it happens in Bell's Palsy. It may take several months for the effect to wear off. Since your facial muscles are paralysed, this means that even if you want to frown, raise your eyebrows or squint, you would not be able to do so. This means that you are left with an expressionless face!

14

Can You Get Rid Of Cellulite By Anti-Cellulite Creams?

Look up any fashion or lifestyle magazines and you will find scores of advertisements for anti-cellulite creams. Earlier nobody had even heard of cellulite but today the magazines have made women very conscious of cellulite. What is a cellulite? It is a fancy name for good old fat under the skin that makes your thighs, buttocks and abdomen have a dimpled appearance like orange peel or cottage cheese.

Cellulite is more visible in obese people but is found in underweight people also. In women, it develops mainly during periods of hormonal changes such as puberty, pregnancy, menopause, etc. The hormone oestrogen aggravates it. Cellulite also depends on genetic factors, diet and smoking. Stress and anxiety also result in cellulite.

Cellulite, therefore, is a complicated problem and to get rid of it one may have to change the entire lifestyle which must also include diet and vigorous exercise. Since most women are reluctant to do that, some companies have started selling 'quick-fix' solutions in the form of anti-cellulite creams. They contain chemicals like aminophylline, retinoids, alpha hydroxy acids and caffeine. The claim is that just rub it and the cellulite will be dissolved.

Prof. John McGrath of the St Johns Institute of Dermatology in London has done great research on this and he confirms that all such creams are absolutely ineffective. Aminophylline is a drug for asthma; retinoids are nothing but derivatives of vitamin A; alpha hydroxy acids are fancy names for acids found in citrus fruits, apples, grapes, tomatoes, apricots and sour milk; and caffeine, as we all know, is found in tea and coffee. There is no evidence that these chemicals can penetrate skin and dissolve fat cells underneath. In fact it is a biological impossibility. Fat in the body can be metabolised but it cannot be dissolved locally. If it were so, what would happen to the dissolved fat – where will it go? The only way to metabolise fat is to consume it by exercise.

Part II

HEALTH AND EXERCISE

15

Can You Get a Flat Abdomen By Doing Sit-Ups Or Abdominal Exercises Alone?

Pot belly is the bane of Indian men. We are continuously exposed to images of models and film stars who have washboard or flat abdomens with rippling muscles. This has created a tremendous inferiority complex amongst the common people. Most men would not mind how their chest or arms look like but a pot belly really bothers them. Cashing on it, exercise gurus and companies making exercise equipment have made them believe that if they do a lot of abdominal exercises like sit-ups or crunches and use their abdominal exercisers, they too will get flat abdomens. Tele-shopping programmes are full of advertisements, which promise you a flat abdomen in just five minutes a day! Do they really work? Contrary to popular belief, they do not work.

Pot bellies amongst the Indian men have as much to do with their genetic constitution as with their great passion for all sorts of fried food like *samosas*, *pooris*, *pakodis* and a myriad of sweets. Most Indians do not want to give up their sedentary lifestyle and eating habits and yet they want a magic exercise or machine that would make them get rid of their pot bellies. Unfortunately, life is not so simple. Scientific research has proved that 'spot reduction' is a myth. There is no way you can reduce fat only from your abdomen. By burning calories through aerobic exercises or dieting, you can reduce fat from all over the body and become thin overall, but there is no way you can selectively reduce the fat on your abdomen.

By doing abdominal exercises like sit-ups or crunches freehand or doing similar movements in abdominal exercise machines, you can make your abdominal muscles (rectus abdominis) stronger and harder but the exercises will not have any effect on the fat on your stomach. If you want to get rid of that pot belly, the fat on the belly is to be burned along with the fat elsewhere in the body and you can do that only by limiting your total calorie intake or by burning calories through vigorous all-round exercise.

16

Can Your Height Increase By Wearing Acupressure Sandals?

You must have seen advertisements of special type of sandals on the television and in magazines, which claim to increase height by acupressure. Various brands are available in the market. They are mostly known by Chinese names like Yoko or Kimi sandals, etc. All those sandals have got a large number of elevated thorn-like projections on them. They claim that if you wear them for just about 15 minutes a day and walk, your height will increase. All such advertisements exploit the basic feelings of insecurity among young men and women. Everybody wants to be taller. Girls develop complexes when they see long-legged models on the ramp or in Miss India competitions. Boys develop a complex when they see tall heroes.

Such products claim to use a dubious Chinese theory called reflexology. They say that the height will increase because the projections on the sandal press on certain acupressure points in the sole, which in turn triggers in the production of growth hormone. But they have never explained on how pressing a certain point on the sole would cause the pituitary gland located in the base of the brain to produce more of growth hormone. The production of growth hormone by the pituitary gland is a self-regulatory and very complex process, and cannot be altered by an external application of pressure or whatever. These sandals hurt the wearer and cause calluses. So far there is not a single case where someone's height has been increased.

We wish life had been so simple. Unfortunately, it is not so. Your height is determined by genetic factors, diet and the exercise you receive in growing years. Injections of growth hormones are available but they are very costly and there are side effects to be reckoned with. Incidentally, the Chinese are said to have discovered this 'secret' centuries ago. Had it been working, they would have made their entire race taller in these centuries! The height of the average Chinese man and woman is still less than that of other races.

17

Can Eating Sweets Lead To Diabetes?

These days many people are rightly afraid of diabetes. In fact some people are so afraid that they stop eating sweets even when they do not have diabetes. The myth is that if you eat sweets, you may get diabetes. Are their fears justified? There are two types of diabetes. In Type I diabetes, there is loss of insulin-producing cells in the pancreas. Type II diabetes results due to insulin resistance or reduced insulin sensitivity combined with reduced insulin secretion. Why it happens is a complex thing; the reasons are genetic too. It is insulin which helps the blood sugar get converted into energy.

Consider a healthy person. All of us know that his weight depends on the calories he takes against the calories he spends. Excess calories would get deposited as fat. Thus eating excess of sweets may result in obesity or other problems but it cannot directly result in diabetes.

What are those other problems? Carbohydrates are complex molecules of simple sugar. In whole food, carbohydrates are bound to fibres, fats, proteins, etc. When we eat whole food, enzymes are released into our digestive tract, which breaks down the complex compounds into their individual components. The body for energy uses the sugar component of the food and any unused amount stored can be used for future needs as fat. When simple sugars/carbohydrates are obtained from whole food, the other natural compounds to which the sugars are bound slow the rate of absorption down dramatically. When the same carbohydrates are obtained in a refined state, large amounts of insulin are released to manage the sugar surge. Too much insulin circulating in the bloodstream and intracellular tissues creates inflammation, which may lead to arterial diseases. Further, the consumption of refined carbohydrates also means that you are not obtaining adequate minerals to maintain normal cellular functions.

People with blood glucose levels that are higher than normal but not yet in the diabetic range have 'pre-diabetes.' If you have pre-diabetes, you have a higher risk of developing Type II diabetes. Such people must be careful about consuming sweets.

18

Does A Woman Become Muscle-Bound If She Practices Weight Training?

Many people believe that women should not do weight training because if they do, they would become muscle-bound like male bodybuilders and lose all their femininity. But it is not so. This myth arises from the images of female professional bodybuilders whom people might have seen.

A man has naturally more muscle mass than a woman due to the higher amount of the male hormone, testosterone, in his body. Now weight training alone cannot increase muscle mass. Becoming stronger by weight training is easy, becoming heavier by weight training is difficult. If you could, however, increase the amount of testosterone in a normal man and if that is accompanied by a protein-rich diet, weight training and adequate rest, increasing the muscle mass becomes easier. Gaining weight (fat) by eating ice creams is easy but gaining muscle weight is difficult. Therefore, those who want quick results, look for short cuts. Since taking additional testosterone could directly affect secondary sexual characteristics and cause medical problems, people take anabolic steroids. Anabolic steroids are synthetic hormones that mimic the action of testosterone, in so far as increasing the muscle mass is concerned, but do not bring about as much change in secondary sexual characteristics. They too have adverse medical effects but they are slow in coming and people tend to ignore them. More muscle mass means you become stronger too and that is why many athletes take anabolic steroids to enhance their performance. Female bodybuilders generally take anabolic steroids.

A normal woman who does not take anabolic steroids need not worry about becoming muscle-bound by weight training. She will not get rippling biceps by doing a few light dumbbells, though she will gain strength in her arms. As her body has less amount of natural testosterone in it, she would not gain muscle mass by weight training alone. Weight training for a woman is in fact beneficial in many other ways. It makes the body stronger and firmer. Above all, it increases the bone density and thereby protects her from osteoporosis later in life.

19

Can Wearing Rudraksha Reduce Blood Pressure?

We are very much aware of the religious significance of *rudraksha* (Elaeocarpus ganitrus). We are not questioning that. However, we must clarify that the ancient Shastras never claimed that *rudraksha* reduced blood pressure. It is a false propaganda by the companies to misguide those who do not have any knowledge of the ancient Shastras. *Rudraksha* was worn as a matter of routine by rishis. Bhagwan Ram himself wore *rudraksha* when he was undergoing the 'vanavasa'; it does not mean that the He (God Himself) was suffering from blood pressure or was liable to suffer from it!

Rudraksha is not the only sacred thing in Hinduism. What *rudraksha* is for the Saivites, the Tulsi beads are for the Vaisnavites. But no such claims are made in respect of Tulsi (Ocimum tenuifolium). Why? The reason is that *rudraksha* has caught the fancy of corrupt companies. *Rudraksha* is somewhat rare and costly; Tusli is cheap and easily available. *Rudraksha* comes in many varieties (with many 'faces') and different virtues are attached to each one of them. On the other hand there is no mystical aura attached with Tusli. A *rudraksha* necklace is prominently seen as a fashion or style statement. Many successful politicians like Indira

Gandhi wore it. Hippies wore it. Tantriks wear it. You can cover the beads in gold if you are rich. All these make *rudraksha* a fashionable product. To wear a *rudraksha* is to make a statement that you 'believe' in traditional things. That is why the companies grabbed it.

There is no medical evidence at all that *rudraksha* helps in reducing blood pressure. It basically cannot. How can a seed worn on the body help in a medical condition? It is not radiating anything; it is not releasing any chemical either. The companies say that *rudraksha* has electromagnetic properties but this is utterly false. It has been repeatedly demonstrated in scientific experiments. The seeds are neither magnetic nor electromagnetic. The claims of medical benefits are all anecdotal. Nobody has ever been cured of blood pressure by wearing *rudraksha* alone.

20

Can Wearing Magnetic Wristbands Help In Relieving Pain Of Arthritis And Other Ailments?

Magnetic wristbands are advertised vigorously on tele-shopping networks. Now you get magnetic bracelets and jewellery; magnetic straps for wrists, ankles and the back; shoe insoles, mattresses and magnetic blankets (blankets with magnets woven into the material); and even water that has been 'magnetised'. Magnetic wristbands are more popular because they are easy to use. All sorts of medical benefits ranging from arthritis, rheumatism, asthma, and HIV to cancer are claimed from the magnetic devices. It is regarded as an outright fraud in the USA and there are restrictions on advertising these products. In India out-of-work actresses and actors are frequently found promoting such products. All you get is testimonials on the television by dubious characters. Well, if that be the criteria of validity then in villages you can surely get testimonials for magical healing by the local *ojha* or *shaman*!

None of the claimed benefits have ever been demonstrated under laboratory conditions. The British Medical Journal and the Journal of American Medical Association have reported experiments on them. Scientists found that subjects who claimed a reduction in pain were aware that they were wearing magnetic bracelets. Whereas, when they were made to wear magnetic bracelets or dummy bracelets without being told, they did not claim any reduction in pain. Obviously it was their belief which made them feel that their pain has reduced; it was not real.

There is not an iota of scientific evidence as to why magnetic bands should work at all. After all they have nothing but a static magnetic field. The field is too weak to have any effect. Some people say that the magnetic field acts on the iron in the blood. They do not know that the iron in blood is ionised and not ferromagnetic. All forms of iron are not magnetic. Everybody knows that steel is not magnetic. Incidentally, scientists who work in nuclear laboratories having particle accelerators are immersed in strong magnetic fields all day long. They never get any benefit whatsoever.

21

Are The New Age Exercise Fads Any Beneficial?

These days a large number of new age exercise fads like Jazz yoga, Power yoga, Aerobic yoga, Stott Pilates, Hydroride, Qigong, Rebounding, Lotte Berk method, Fitness Boot Camp, Tai Chi, BOSU, Masala bhangra and Chakra dance are being marketed by magazines. Fashionable gymnasiums have sprung even in small towns where they charge the customers heavily for such fads. It is all clever marketing. They do not offer any additional benefits over cheaper traditional forms of exercises.

Westerners have made a joke of yoga. Jazz music was born by a mixture of African music with western classical music; jazz yoga is a mixture of a bit of yoga with western dance where postures are made in a playful way! Power yoga is a fast-paced callisthenics workout with yoga postures thrown in. Aerobic yoga is aerobics with yoga thrown in. Pilates is a mystical thing, which claims to use the mind to control the core postural muscles. Stott Pilates is a modern version of the old method of using mats, some light resistance and balance equipment. Hydroride is an exercise-cycle driven in water for added resistance. Qigong and Tai Chi are Chinese exercise systems involving coordination of breathing with physical postures. Rebounding is a jumping exercise done on a small trampoline. Lotte Berk was a dancer who developed a method, quite similar to the Pilates. Fitness Boot Camp is nothing but old military training involving running, lifting weights, etc. in a fashionable way. BOSU is an inflated hemispherical rubber ball used for balance training. Masala bhangra is simply old aerobics done to bhangra beat with some bhangra moves thrown in. Chakra dance is free dancing with some mystic mumbo-jumbo.

Scientifically speaking, exercise has only three basic forms: cardio, resistance and endurance. Whichever way you move your limbs, you are doing one of these exercises only. Whether you do bhangra or jump on trampoline; your body understands it as cardio workout only. The new fads may be more fun but do not offer any additional benefit over other forms of exercises.

22

Are Antibacterial Soaps Any Better Than Plain Soaps?

Most of the so-called antibacterial soaps advertise that they kill 99% of the bacteria and thus protect your family better than plain soaps. Some of them go to the extent of telling you that your child can take a bath once with an antibacterial soap and then go on playing in dirt and filth all day long because the soap offers continued protection. It is all unethical marketing. Even if soap were to kill every single bacterium on your hands, once the soap is washed off, no chemical remains there to kill any germ which might come later. It is impossible for the chemical to remain on your hands. The fact is that they cannot kill all germs. Allison Aiello of the University of Michigan School of Public Health has shown that antibacterial soaps at formulations sold do not remove any more bacteria from the hands during washing than plain soaps. Further, washing hands with an antibacterial soap was found to be no more effective in preventing infectious illnesses than plain soaps.

Several antibacterial soaps go by the name of the original antiseptic. One antiseptic contains chloroxylenol. However, the soap by its name does not contain this chemical. It contains triclosan. Another antiseptic contains chlorhexidine and cetrimide. The soap with its name, however, contains triclosan only. There is no doubt about the value of chlorxylenol, chlorhexidine or cetrimide as antiseptics. It is triclosan that is in doubt. In the first place the companies mislead you by using the original name and making you believe that the soaps too might be containing the same chemicals. But it is not so. Secondly, triclosan is not effective as an antiseptic when it is used in the concentrations found in soaps. Higher concentrations would make the soap harmful to skin.

Because of the way triclosan kills the bacteria, mutations can happen at the targeted site. Aiello says a mutation could mean that the triclosan can no longer get to the target site to kill the bacteria. The Michigan team also found that triclosan could make many bacteria like E-Coli resistant to drugs like amoxicillin.

23

Does Reiki Really Have Any Miraculous Health Benefits?

Reiki is a miraculous system of healing that has become quite popular. In Reiki the healer touches your body and claims that 'healing energy' flows from his palm into your body and that would heal you. The meaning of the Japanese word 'reiki' is 'unseen energy'. The 'ki' in this word is the same as 'chi' in acupuncture and martial arts. Reiki claims that there is a 'universal life energy' which can be tapped by the reiki master and then channelled into the body of the sick person. Advanced reiki masters claim that they can transfer that energy from a distance too. Where is this energy, what is it and how can the reiki master tap it? There is no answer. Science does not admit of any energy other than electrical, mechanical, chemical, gravitational or nuclear; the 'universal life energy' is not one of them.

A Japanese called Mikao Usui developed Reiki. Usui claimed in 1922 that by a mystical revelation he had gained this knowledge and spiritual power.

It should be obvious that the whole thing is as fanciful as faith healing by controversial men like pastor Benny Hinn. They invoke the power of Jesus; reiki invokes the power of 'universal life energy'.

Dr William Jarvis of National Council Against Health Fraud in Massachusetts has done research on reiki and has shown that there is no evidence that Reiki's clinical effects, if at all there are some, are due to anything other than suggestion. If you believe in miracles and if the miracle-worker keeps on telling you that you are feeling better, you may be led into believing that you are feeling better unless your problem is really serious. And those who have serious problems do not go to a reiki practitioner. Most people who go to reiki practitioners suffer from problems which are largely psychological in character, and they start feeling better by the mere fact of someone being sympathetic to their woes. In fact some reiki practitioners do encourage their clients to consult a medical doctor for serious conditions.

24

Can You Really Get Any Health Benefit By Pranic Healing?

Pranic healing claims to be a system of healing techniques that utilises 'prana' to balance, harmonise and transform the body's energy processes. 'Prana' is a Sanskrit word that means, 'life force'. They say that prana is similar to what the Chinese call as Chi in acupuncture and martial arts, and what the Old Testament calls the 'Breath of Life'.

No hoax could be bigger than this because this is a modern-day forgery on some ancient concepts. Ancient texts of India and ayurveda do admit of prana but they do not say that you can manipulate it. They speak of five pranas which leave the body when you die, i.e. they are not a part of your physical body. In ayurveda, health concerns with the well being of the physical body. It does not touch the prana or the atma as these are not material.

This means that there is no connection of pranic healing with ayurveda. They are merely using a Sanskrit word to confuse people. A man called Choa Kok Sui developed this mix up. He is a clever man. Look at what he has to say in www.pranichealing.org: 'Pranic Healing is not intended to replace orthodox medicine, but rather to complement it. If symptoms persist or the ailment is severe, please consult immediately a Medical Doctor and a Certified Pranic Healer.'

In pranic healing they do not even touch your body. Their central belief is that there is a bio-electromagnetic field known as the aura, which contains the mould and blueprint of the physical body. This bioplasmic body absorbs life energy and distributes it to the organs and glands. Diseases first appear as energetic disruptions in the energy field before manifesting as ailments in the physical body. Pranic healing claims to influence this life energy to bring about a healthier physical body. The catch is that electromagnetic things are measurable and nothing like this has ever been found. Ayurveda and the Hindu tradition take the pranas as supra-material things; pranic healing takes it to be material and yet fails to show it.

25

Can Smoking Low-Nicotine Cigarettes Help In Reducing Chances Of Cancer?

This is a very popular misconception amongst smokers who have somehow been convinced that smoking could be injurious to health. They are torn between two desires; the desire to quit and the desire to continue the pleasure of smoking. Since many of them have heard of nicotine as the chief culprit, they think that if they smoke what are marketed as low-nicotine cigarettes, they can get the best of both worlds; the pleasure of smoking as well as freedom from the risk of cancer. Unfortunately, it is not so. It is a very unethical marketing trick of the tobacco companies.

Through their advertisements they have been trying to reassure the smokers that low-nicotine cigarettes are safer than they were in the past. They say that they reduce the cancer-causing tars by two methods. First, they use a different part of the tobacco plant, and second, they introduce filters to block the tar from getting into the lungs. Then they started saying that they are selling 'light' or 'mild' cigarettes which would dump even less tar into your lungs. In the first place, scientific experiments have shown that filters are not at all capable of doing what they claim to do.

There is a simple catch in this. Cigarette smokers smoke for the pleasure that they get from nicotine. If you reduce the quantity of nicotine in cigarettes, you do not get the same pleasure. Nicotine is an addictive thing. In fact that is how people become smokers. A certain level of nicotine is required to continue the addiction. If the smokers do not have the will power to stop smoking, they will somehow get this dose of nicotine. Now cigarette smoking has two variables; basically, how hard you suck and how frequently you suck. When low-nicotine cigarette is given to a smoker, he, even without his knowing, starts sucking harder and more frequently. Thus he gets the same amount of nicotine, which he would have got with a regular cigarette. Not only that, by sucking more, you inhale more of carbon monoxide that does further harm.

26

Can Taking Large Doses Of Vitamin C Help In Preventing Common Cold?

Since the 1970s, it has been believed by many that Vitamin C helps in cold. How did this myth come into existent? The myth was propagated by Linus Pauling in his book *Vitamin C and the Common Cold.* It took scientists over 30 years to debunk the myth.

In a survey of scientific studies spanning more than two decades and including more than 11,000 people, those who took 200 mg of vitamin C daily suffered from as much cold as those who took no supplements. The vitamin also failed to have a substantial effect on the length and severity of a person's cold.

The latest survey, compiled results from 30 different studies around the world, concluded that only people who were exposed to exceptionally high levels of stress, such as marathon runners, skiers and soldiers on subarctic exercises, had fewer colds as a result of taking the vitamin. Among them, a daily supplement of vitamin C reduced the chances of catching a cold by half.

Harri Hemilä at Helsinki University, who led the survey, said that for most people the cold-preventing effect of taking daily vitamin C supplements was so slight that it was not worth the effort or expense. 'It doesn't make sense to take vitamin C 365 days a year to lessen the chance of catching a cold,' he said.

There is no need of taking any supplement of vitamin C if you are taking a healthy diet. The current recommended daily dose of vitamin C is just 60 mg. A large glass of orange juice contains nearly 100 mg and taking more than 500 mg of vitamin C at any one time provides no advantage. Any excess of vitamin C is simply lost through non-absorption or urination. In fact, people with kidney diseases should avoid vitamin C supplements.

The vitamin C episode shows that if business interests are involved, even scientists could dole out wrong information.

27

Can Calcium In Toothpaste Make Your Teeth Stronger And Help Fight Germs For 12 Hours?

Toothpastes have a huge market. Hence the competition is stiff and they are always trying new gimmicks to lure the customers. We should try and understand some basic things about toothpastes. Toothpastes are good for oral hygiene. But most of the benefits of toothpaste come from the action of brushing in the presence of a foaming substance and not from any ingredient in the toothpastes. Most toothpaste has a foaming agent called sodium lauryl sulphate. Incidentally, this is also the foaming agent in shampoos and shaving creams. The foaming agent is mixed with polishing agents like tricalcium phosphate. Tricalcium phosphate is usually obtained from bone ash; strictly speaking it is not a vegetarian product. It cleanses and polishes the teeth in exactly the same manner in which powders clean utensils. Then there are moisteners like glycerin and sorbitol; sweeteners like saccharine; and binding agents like starch, gum, etc.

All other ingredients, which are mixed in various toothpastes, are essentially marketing gimmicks. Some of them claim to have an antibacterial substance like triclosan. This has no effect in the concentrations used in toothpastes. It has been found useless even in the so-called antibacterial soaps also. Some of them have clove oil. Clove oil reduces pain in teeth only if it is applied for a long time (usually a piece of cotton soaked in it is pressed on the tooth). A toothpaste remains in contact only for a short time and the concentration of the oil is very low. Some claim to have calcium to make your teeth stronger. As we saw, all toothpastes have tricalcium phosphate and this can work as a calcium supplement only if it is taken internally. Do the companies expect you to eat toothpaste? Some also claim to have 'active salt'. In chemistry there is nothing called 'active salt'. Adding salt to toothpaste does not enhance its quality. Then some claim that they 'fight decay' for several hours. This cannot happen because the toothpaste is rinsed off. No chemical remains after that, and the tooth decay will start the moment you eat something after brushing.

28

Is The Morning Walker Machine Of Any Use?

You must have certainly seen the advertisement of the so-called morning walker machine. It is a small machine with footrests for your feet. All you have to do is lie down and place your feet on the footrests. An electric motor rocks the footrest on the platform in a sideways motion. Since your lower torso is elevated, the rocking of your feet shakes your lower half. Now, the advertisement claims that spending 15 minutes on the machine is equivalent to walking 10,000 steps. Hence all the benefits that one could possibly get from walking 10,000 steps are obtained by lying on the machine.

The company is cheating the consumers in broad daylight is one thing; what is more disturbing is that many people are taken in by such fraudulent claims.

When you walk or run, your muscles work and you propel your legs forward. That can happen only when the muscles work. So when you move the legs forward, you are not dragging them on the ground. The legs have to be lifted a little in the air to facilitate their movements. Lifting legs in the air against gravity means your muscles have to work for lifting the weight of your legs. Then there is friction between your feet and the ground.

Don't you realise it? As you know, walking on sand is more difficult than walking on road. Why; because sand offers a higher friction to the feet than the road. To overcome this friction, the muscles have to work. It is due to such work that walking becomes an exercise. When muscles work, the heart has to pump more blood and you get the beneficial effects of exercise.

In the morning walker machine, your muscles are not doing any work at all. The electric motor is basically shaking them sideways against the friction of the platform. Even if you are there for an hour, you will not get any exercise at all. Just think, will you get any exercise if someone were to shake your hands?

29

How Effective Are Pain Relief Creams?

The market is flooded with numerous pain relief creams. The punch line for one of them is '*dard mitaye chutkiyon mein*'. The product basically claims that it will get rid of your pain in a matter of seconds. How far is this true?

Pain is the result of some inflammation. Thus inflammation is to be tackled by non-steroid anti-inflammatory drugs (NSAIDs). Steroids are generally injected under medical supervision and hence we will discuss only the NSAIDs. The drugs commonly used are diclofenac and nimesulide. These drugs penetrate the skin very slowly. Studies that have been carried out at the Department of Pharmacology, AIIMS found that the peak level of the drugs is reached only between 90 to 120 minutes of application. Older formulations that used methyl salicylate or trolamine salicylate are equally slow.

Many of the creams have topical anesthetics and oils in them. Topical anesthetics like lidocaine are used in such creams as they merely deaden the nerve endings on the skin. They do nothing towards the cause of pain. They act very fast but the action is short-lived. Some creams use menthol also. This is a weak anesthetic. Some creams use oil of wintergreen. This has no function other than opening the pores somewhat.

Thus we see that the actual relief of pain by the application of a topical cream in an inflamed area cannot be realised before 90 minutes in any case. Before that, all you get is a little anesthetic action, which does nothing towards the cause of inflammation. Hence the claim of '*dard mitaye chutkiyon mein*' is false.

Topical application is no substitute for internal treatment.

The famous Tiger Balm contains menthol, camphor, dementholised mint oil, Cajuput oil, Clove oil and Cassia oil. The anti-inflammatory agent is Cassia oil; others exert only a mild anesthetic or soothing action. There is no way it can work in minutes.

30

Can Reading In Poor Light Affect Your Eyesight And Other Myths Related To Vision?

For generations, mothers have been insisting that kids must read in bright light otherwise their eyesight will be affected. There are a host of other myths regarding eyesight to the effect that if you do such-and-such, you will be obliged to wear glasses. Wearing glasses mean that you have a refractory defect in which the lens of your eye is not able to focus the image on the retina by itself because the eyeball has misshaped. The problem is solved by adding another lens, that is, the lens of the spectacles. The reasons for refractory defects are complex and could be hereditary too.

Reading in poor light may be uncomfortable; your pupils will dilate to let more light in. But there is no way it can cause a refractory defect. Poor light does not bring the lens or the eyeball into the picture at all. The lens cannot do anything to bring in more light. It is only the aperture which has to be widened. Widening the aperture does not affect the lens or the eyeball. The other myth is that if you read too much or do much of intricate work like embroidery, you will need glasses. Once again, detailed work may tire your eyes faster but it is not going to introduce any defect in the lens. The eyes cannot be likened to an ordinary machine which wears out faster with greater use. Human organs are marvellous; they last a lifetime. Does not your heart beat continuously till you die? Then it is believed by many people that some eye exercises can ward off glasses. William Bates had popularised the exercises in his book *Perfect Sight Without Glasses*. This book was published in 1920 and reflected the knowledge available in that era. Medical science has made enormous progress since then and the notions of Bates have been rejected. Sitting close to the TV or brightness of light in the TV room is a matter of personal preference; none of these will introduce a refractory defect.

31

Are Sauna Baths Beneficial?

European lifestyle has become very popular among the Indians. Sauna is one of them. Most of the costly spas offer saunas. What is a sauna? Sauna is the Finnish word for bath. A sauna is a small room in which you can be exposed to wet or dry heat. The Finnish people invented it centuries ago. You must understand that the Europeans did not wash their bodies regularly because they thought that water carried disease into the body through the skin. That is why perfume was used to suppress the body odour. It was in such an era that the steam bath was invented.

For the participants it was also a social affair in which they disrobed and sat together to relax and chat. Some hotel sauna facilities and especially cruise ships and ferries have an area where refreshments (often alcoholic) are served in conjunction with the sauna/pool area.

There is no medically proven benefit of sauna. The claims that it is refreshing or relaxing are highly subjective. It is a pure myth that sweating removes toxins from the body. The sauna or any steam bath for that matter cannot take the place of regular washing of the body. Sweating in steam does not remove the dirt from your body. But in an era, for those who did not wash their bodies regularly and when people did not have running hot water in their houses, the sauna gave an opportunity to get some sort of bath. In the modern age, when even the Europeans in cold climates bathe regularly, a steam bath has little relevance. Hence, it survives only as a relic which has been patronised by the hotel industry as a mechanism for making fools of customers.

Unless the humidity and temperature are precisely controlled, a sauna can be a painful experience and may result in heat prostration. You lose a considerable amount of sweat in it and mistake it as weight loss. This loss is made up as soon as you drink water.

32

Does Red Wine Have Any Great Medicinal Value?

Of late red wine is being touted as a sophisticated drink with great medicinal values. Is there any truth in it? Wine is being consumed all over the world since millennia. But nobody ever said so before. Then how come this belief has arisen now? Scientists claim that it is a marketing ploy of the companies, which manufacture red wine to promote their product. Indians, for example, traditionally used to drink largely whisky and rum. When the wine-making companies wanted to grab a share of the market, they had to propagate some myths. This is it. They even concocted a story that red wine contains a substance called reserveratrol, which claims to have anti-ageing and anti-carcinogenic effects besides being good for the heart.

Dr Tim Sanders of the USDA Agricultural Research Service in North Carolina has shown that the evidence about the benefits of reserveratrol is shaky. Secondly, reserveratrol is not only present in red wine, it is found in much larger quantities in things as simple as the lowly peanut. Half an ounce of peanuts has as much reserveratrol as six ounces of wine. Nobody ever claimed such benefits from peanuts. Thirdly, the amount of reserveratrol in food items, whether peanuts or red wine, is too small to have any therapeutic effect. If you consume them in large quantities then the bad effects would outweigh the claimed good effects. The companies had got some tests conducted on mice that were given pure reserveratrol. The dose was equivalent to 20 bottles of wine per day! You can well imagine what would happen to a man if he drank 20 bottles per day!

After this discovery, the companies latched onto another chemical called endetholin in wine, which claims to have good effect on the heart. This was debunked by Professor Roger Corder of the Queen Mary College, London, who opined, "The changes that alcohol causes are so modest that you would not in your right mind believe that they could protect you from heart disease."

33

Is There Any Significance Of The So-Called Cooling Crystals In Toothpaste?

You certainly must have seen the advertisement of Colgate MaxFresh gel toothpaste featuring movie stars. The claim is that it is the first and only toothpaste infused with cooling crystals that dissolve in the mouth completely upon brushing, thus releasing an intense rush of breath freshening power.

Hence, the USP of the toothpaste is the so-called cooling crystals. You can look up any book of chemistry and you would not find anything called 'cooling crystal'. If you want, you can search in 'google' but you would not find anything. Then what are those cooling crystals?

The active ingredient in the cooling crystals is nothing but menthol. There is nothing great about it. Menthol is extracted from the plant Mentha arvensis. The plant is incidentally Indian. Menthol is the solid constituent of mint oil, to which its characteristic odour is due, and was formerly known as peppermint camphor. Menthol crystals are cooling, refreshing and have a pleasant smell of mint. They are often used in cosmetics, salves, balms, medicated creams, throat lozenges, toothpaste, mouthwash, gum, foot sprays, pain relief or cooling body products, shampoos, conditioners, liniments, shaving creams, oral or throat sprays, compresses, medicated oils and cooling gels.

What they have done is prepared a form of menthol that is soluble in water. Normally menthol is soluble in alcohol and essential oils only. They have made a composition of menthol with a substance called isopulegol, which enables it to be dissolved in water in the mouth. There is nothing new about the use of menthol in toothpastes. This company has only packaged it differently. As far as the mouth is concerned, it does not make any difference whether it has got menthol in oil base or water-soluble base. After all, oils like clove oil have been added in toothpastes in oil form only. It is an example of how old wine can be sold in a new bottle.

34

Is The So-Called Detoxification Of The Body Really Possible?

One of the preferred topics of lifestyle magazines is detoxification. It is very fashionable to claim that the body acquires toxins (whatever they may mean) and one must get rid of the toxins by fasting, drinking fruit juices, vegetable juices, herbal teas and taking special baths or electromagnetic treatment. But how exactly these substances will help in removing toxins is never explained.

They have never been able to answer one simple question. The body has its own mechanism of removing toxic substances. It is one of the major functions of the liver, lower gastrointestinal tract and kidneys. They remove toxic substances at their own rate, which are nothing but metabolic wastes. As long as you are eating things which are fit for human consumption, the metabolic wastes will be removed by the excretory organs.

Dr John Emsley, chemical scientist in UK and Prof. Martin Wiseman, visiting professor of human nutrition, University of Southampton have shown that detoxification remedies are a waste of money whereas a glass of water and an early night's sleep are far more beneficial. They reiterate that the body detoxifies itself as long as the liver and kidneys are functioning properly. If you are stressed out, it is not because of the toxins accumulated in the body. The tired body can be rehydrated with ordinary tap water and refreshed with a good night's sleep. There is no way you can speed up the elimination process by drinking fancy bottled water or sipping herbal teas. The liver and kidneys work at their own rates and you can neither slow them down nor accelerate their functioning.

Part III

DIET AND NUTRITION

35

Can 'An Apple A Day Really Keep The Doctor Away'?

Who has not heard of this old adage? This is a classic example of how an ignorance of the distant past has continued even in the modern age. The medieval Europeans knew only one fruit, the apple. When they found new fruits, even they were named after apples only, such as pineapple, custard apple, etc. It was, therefore, natural for them to attribute properties to this fruit. In the modern age, when all sorts of healthy food are available, this myth has no basis.

After all, what does the apple contain? An apple has nothing more nutritious in it, which other fruits do not have. Actually there is a historical reason of the myth's existence. The traditional European diet in the medieval period was practically all meat – they hardly ate any vegetables and thus got very little dietary fibre. Hence, constipation was a major problem. Many other problems followed constipation, such as acidity, heartburn, stomach ache, headache, colorectal and anorectal problems, haemorrhoids and even colon cancer, etc. In that age, apple was a good source of dietary fibre. Hence, those who ate apples were less likely to suffer from such problems. That is how this myth was born.

It should be very clear that apple or for that matter any fruit does not contain any vitamins or minerals which will prevent a medical condition other than those described earlier. In the modern age, we have numerous sources of dietary fibre; there is no reason to exalt the apple. Eating fruits will not save you from, say, even the common cold.

Fruits are required to make a good balanced diet; keep their importance to that only. A good balanced diet needs to be supplemented with a healthy lifestyle. Merely eating good food is not enough. If you want to ward off diseases, you must maintain a healthy lifestyle, which must involve physical activities too.

36

Can You Lose Weight By Drinking Honey And Lemon In Warm Water?

This is one of the oldest myths of dieting. The advice given is that you should drink honey and lemon drops in warm water on an empty stomach in the morning. The fact is that nobody has ever lost any weight by this. The scientific fact is that it is not possible either.

Honey contains slightly less sugar than ordinary table sugar because it has some water in it. Honey has 82.12% sugar and 17.10% of water besides a little protein and fibre. Table sugar is 99.91% sugar. A hundred grams of sugar gives 390 calories; 100 grams of honey gives 300 calories. But you are not going to lose any weight by substituting sugar with honey because if you are using honey as a sweetener, you will tend to use more honey to get the same degree of sweetness. Let us understand one thing very clearly. The stomach understands only chemistry. For the stomach there is no difference between the sugar in honey and sugar in table sugar. That leaves the lemon juice. The myth says that it dissolves excess fat. That is plainly ridiculous. The fat deposits under the skin cannot be dissolved. They can only be converted into energy should you require energy for doing vigorous exercise.

Lemon juice as we all know has citric acid in it besides some vitamin C. Vitamin C has no role to play in weight loss. Citric acid is a simple acid. How can it dissolve fat that is deposited under the skin? After absorption in the stomach it is eventually metabolised and eliminated through the kidneys as sodium carbonate. And if value were to be attached to citric acid, it can be found in many other things like oranges, pineapples, tomatoes, gooseberries, strawberries and currants too. Did anybody ever tell you that a sherbet of honey with orange juice could help in weight loss? As for warm water, the temperature of water has no bearing on how sugar or citric acid will be digested. Take the mixture warm or cold, there is no difference.

37

Can Taking Muesli In Breakfast Make You Highly Energetic?

Muesli is a breakfast cereal. The advertisement of a popular brand states that a woman who takes this will get superhuman energy: 'Morning walk. Drop daughter off at school. Pick up a colleague. Back to back meetings. Lunch with mom. Send presentation to the manager for approval. Pick up daughter and son. Drop daughter for bharatnatyam classes. Drop son for cricket practice. Pick up husband from airport. Make dinner. Go to husband's office party. Call sister-in-law in US.'

If this mythical woman of the advertisement has such tremendous energy, it is fine. The objectionable fact is that all this is attributed to muesli. This claim is absolutely unscientific. Muesli does not consist of anything other than oats, corn and wheat flakes, almonds, figs, dates, jaggery and honey. There is nothing special about them. Jaggery and honey are nothing but sources of simple sugar. Dates are also predominantly (73.5%) sources of sugars. Figs have 63.5% sugars. They have very little proteins or fats. You could as well take sugar in the form of much cheaper table sugar added to your tea or whatever. Sugar goes directly into the bloodstream and gives instant energy but the effect does not last long. Complex carbohydrates take a longer time to break down and hence they give energy for a longer time. Corn and wheat are complex carbohydrates. If it is argued that cornflakes or wheat flakes in muesli give energy for a longer time, the same effect can be obtained by eating a chapati, 'makki di roti' or any other traditional source of complex carbohydrates. There is nothing special about the wheat or corn used in corn and wheat flakes. Almonds have good fats and proteins but the question is how many almonds are found in one serving of muesli? In any case, if at all one has to take the benefit of almonds; one could munch them just like that any time during the day. Adding them to breakfast cereal does not make them of any special value. Thus muesli offers nothing extra that one cannot get from his regular breakfast.

38

Is Spinach Really A Good Source Of Iron As It Is Believed To Be?

Ever since your childhood you must have heard from your mother that one must eat spinach because it is a very good source of iron. That is where all the dieticians and magazines flounder. Spinach has iron in it. 100 gram (1/2 cup) of cooked spinach has about 3 mg irons. Compare that to the daily iron needs of a man (8 mg) and woman (18 mg). That makes spinach sound like a great source of iron.

But merely having iron in it is not enough. The question is whether it is made available to the body. In other words, what is the bioavailability of iron in spinach? The 'choona' (slaked lime) in 'paan' is calcium hydroxide. Does it mean that choona can be used as a calcium supplement? No, because calcium hydroxide cannot be absorbed by the human body. The same thing happens with spinach. Unfortunately, spinach has a huge amount of oxalate, a compound that gives spinach its characteristic taste. The oxalate binds with iron to form a compound called ferrous oxalate, a compound that you cannot digest; hence the iron passes all the way through your digestive tract. There is another compound called phytic acid, which is present in the spinach and also binds with it and lowers its absorption. The oxalate is also bound to most of the calcium in spinach. Our gut absorbs a miserable 1% of the iron and 5% of the calcium in spinach.

The nutrient composition of spinach is not the only factor to consider when it comes to iron availability. Foods eaten alongside spinach can also affect iron absorption. Tannins in tea, for example, have also been shown to interfere with iron absorption. In some instances, a cup of tea can lower the availability of non-heme iron by as much as 60%.

Thus it would not be advisable to depend on spinach as the sole source of iron. It can supplement other sources but would not be enough by itself.

39

Do New Age Diet Fads Really Work?

Dieting is one of the most popular fads in the world. A large number of diet fads have been invented in the US. Lifestyle magazines in India do nothing but copy American ideas by propagating these fads and many affluent women have fallen prey to them.

The Atkins diet restricts carbohydrates severely and pumps proteins and fats. The idea is that the body should be deprived of carbohydrates so that the body is forced to burn stored fat. The General Motors diet for a week keeps you on fruits and vegetables for three days; bananas and milk on the fourth day; the next two days are for beef and vegetables; and the seventh day is for brown rice and vegetables. The South Beach diet emphasises on the consumption of what they call 'good' carbohydrates and fats.

Scientists have found that the claims regarding all such fads have been made without adequate research and clinical trials. All that they have in their support are testimonials but not scientifically proven results. As you can see, all such diets are nutritionally unbalanced. That is their biggest problem. Anybody can lose weight temporarily by not eating anything or eating an unbalanced diet, but that is not a solution. When you return to your old eating pattern, the weight also returns. When high-protein diets are found to work, the result is only temporary because caloric intake is limited to 800 to 1,200 calories a day, which is just not enough to meet the average adult's nutritional needs. In any case, no dieter, unless he is crazy, can maintain such unnatural diet patterns for long. If they do, they will develop other medical complications.

Diet fads become popular because people desire miracles – something that would make them lose 15 pounds in a week. Unfortunately there are no miracles in real life.

There are only three components to a scientific way of dieting: eating a balanced diet comprising all the necessary things like carbohydrates, proteins and fats; eating fewer calories; and spending more calories by exercise. Only this can maintain a permanent weight loss.

40

Is Eating Walnuts Or Almonds Good For The Brain?

In India, there is a very popular belief that eating walnut or almond is good for the brain. In fact, earlier all those who did 'brainy' work like lawyers, scholars, students, etc. were routinely fed these by their wives or mothers. Elsewhere in the world there is a long list of food items that are supposed to be good for the brain. But remember one thing: had it really been possible for someone to improve his intellectual capacity by eating a certain food item, no rich man in human history would have been stupid. This in itself proves the point. You can take an academically poor student and feed him as much walnuts as you please. Would he ever become a brilliant student by that? Actually, the reason behind attributing this property to walnuts is simple. Walnuts do look like human brains. Then someone might have thought that eating walnuts or almonds could help the brain – thus the myth was born.

People attribute the same properties to oily fish like salmon or fresh tuna. Once again the fact is that in many parts of the world, people have been eating salmon and fresh tuna for ages – have they all become intelligent?

It is true that omega-3 acids make up a part of the outer membrane of brain cells. It is also true that walnuts and salmon do contain omega-3 acids. That, however, does not mean that eating omega-3 acids can make one intelligent. Intelligence is the result of many factors and not simply the number of brain cells. If we go by that logic then the person with a large head should be more intelligent.

Have you not heard of poor impoverished children who are very intelligent? Intelligence depends on learning, information processing, interest, attention, dedication and so on. It is not a diet dependent thing. The brain is different from other organs because it is cognitive. Calcium deficiency may result in weak bones but omega-3 deficiency will not result in a stupid man.

41

Is There Anything Particularly Good About The So-Called Probiotic Ice Cream?

Some companies like Amul have started marketing what they call probiotic ice creams. It is coming to India a little late. The probiotic ice creams were first sold in Sweden in 1997. It was never a success and yet it took 8 years for the Indians to copy a useless thing and make tall claims about their benefits ranging from acne to heart diseases and even cancer.

What is probiotic? It is just a fancy name for a food item in which they have artificially added some beneficial bacteria. As you know, there are some useful bacteria that live in our guts. The most famous of them is the lactobacillus (LAB). They convert carbohydrates into lactic acid. They make yoghurt (dahi) from milk. Now nobody needs to be told the health benefits of yoghurt. We have been eating dahi for centuries. Even those people who cannot digest milk due to enzyme deficiency can digest yoghurt. It is so useful that they are made even in capsule form – Becelac. For example, if the useful bacteria in your guts are killed following a long course of antibiotics, you can take the capsules and they would replenish them. Otherwise you would be obliged to eat a lot of yoghurt.

There is no dispute about the beneficiary effect of lactobacillus. The dispute is about adding them to other food items. It does no harm but it does not make it a wonder food either. Whatever benefit you are supposed to get from eating a probiotic ice cream, you can get by eating a bowl of yoghurt which is much cheaper and has other health benefits too. You can have low-fat yoghurt but you cannot have low-fat ice cream. Or if it comes to that you could take even a capsule. This should not be a problem for Indians. A Swedish man might not get yoghurt easily but here it is available at every corner. Indians should not fall into such marketing traps. Any probiotic food will not give you anything more than what yoghurt gives.

42

Is The Costly Green Tea Any Better Than The Ordinary Black Tea?

It is quite fashionable to exalt green tea over the ordinary black tea, which we have been consuming for long in this country. Green tea is the national drink of China and Japan, and they make it ceremoniously in five star hotels, i.e. inviting society ladies to witness tea ceremonies by imported experts. Above all, it is costlier. For the Indians, anything that is costly must be better. Many claims have been made regarding the health benefits of green tea. Lifestyle magazines abound in them.

Green tea was claimed to help in cardiovascular diseases as well as cancer. The Food and Drug Administration in the USA did research on that. On June 30, 2005 in response to 'Green Tea and Reduced Risk of Cancer Health Claim', they stated: "FDA concludes that there is no credible evidence to support qualified health claims for green tea consumption and a reduced risk of gastric, lung, colon/rectal, oesophageal, pancreatic, ovarian and combined cancers. Thus, FDA is denying these claims." On May 9, 2006 in response to 'Green Tea and Reduced Risk of Cardiovascular Disease', they concluded: "There is no credible evidence to support qualified health claims for green tea or green tea extract and a reduction of a number of risk factors associated with cardiovascular diseases." Jane Higden of Linus Pauling Institute also states: "Although numerous observational studies have examined the relationships between tea consumption and the risks of cardiovascular disease and cancer, there is no conclusive evidence that high intakes of tea are protective in humans."

Most people do not know that the only difference between green tea and black tea is that black tea is made from fermented tea leaves. The alleged superiority of green tea rested on the belief that it has an antioxidant called epigallocatechin gallate (EGCg). They claimed that it changed to other compounds when fermented. Impartial research has found that black tea contains chemicals like theaflavins and thearubigens, which have the same function.

43

Are Fancy Energy Drinks Like Red Bull Of Any Value At All?

Red Bull is an energy drink marketed by a Thailand based company, and later popularised by an Austrian company. Its advertisements claim that it gives instant energy and combats both physical and mental fatigue. It is widely consumed by sportspersons who think that it helps them perform better and all those youth who think that it will help them party harder. The drink is intended to taste like mixed berries, and is commonly used as mixer in alcoholic drinks such as vodka. Over one billion cans of the drink are sold in the world every year. Incidentally, it was first popularised by truck drivers who claimed that they could stay awake longer with this.

Scientists like Dr Mark Kantor of the University of Maryland and the Swedish National Food Administration (SNFA) have thoroughly debunked its claims. The only source of instant energy for the human body is sugar. Red Bull has nothing mysterious in it. A 250 ml can of Red Bull contains nearly an ounce or 27 grams of sugar. Thus if you feel any energy after drinking Red Bull, it has come from nothing but the full ounce of sugar in it. You could have as well taken sherbet or *nimbu-paani* with an equal amount of sugar (5 tsp) for the same energy and saved a lot of money. The other thing which Red Bull has is 80 mg of caffeine. This is less than what you get in a cup of coffee. You could as well drink a cup of coffee. It has two more things, 1000 mg of taurine and 600 mg of glucoronolactone. Taurine is a substance found in the bile of oxen (scientific name Bos Taurus) – hence the name. Thus it is not a vegetarian substance. Glucoronolactone is a byproduct of the metabolism of glucose in human liver. The rest is just carbonated water like any other soft drink. Taurine and glucoronolactone were claimed to combat fatigue but no evidence has been found in support of this. The SNFA has found that it is dangerous to consume it with alcohol or after strenuous exercise.

44

Is Genetically Modified (GM) Food Perfectly Safe To Eat?

Genetically modified (GM) foods are those foodstuffs that are produced from plants or organisms which have got their genome altered by genetic engineering. The original purpose of the research was to produce variety that have certain special qualities, such as tomatoes that would not rot easily, maize, soya bean, rapeseed and cotton that would be more resistant to insects as well as herbicides. They may be good for increased production but contrary to what the governments say, GM food or crops are not at all safe.

The most exhaustive research in this field is done by J. M. Smith, who has shown in his book *Genetic Roulette: The Documented Health Risks of Genetically Engineered Foods* that GM foods are inherently unsafe.

Consider GM soya bean, for example. Many people are allergic to soya beans. After GM soya bean was introduced in the UK, the allergies immediately increased by 50%. It was found that the GM transformation process increased the amount of allergens like trypsin inhibitor in soya bean by 27%. The allergy study identified irritable bowel syndrome, digestion problems, chronic fatigue, headaches, lethargy, and skin complaints including acne and eczema as the problems caused by GM soya bean.

Some GM plants are so made that they themselves produce an insecticide called BT toxin (from the bacterium Bacillus Thuringiensis). The BT corn, for example, produces it. The idea was that there would be no need of spraying the plant with insecticides and they would be able to protect themselves from insects. It sounded very fine on paper but clearly missed the point that while you try to wash off a sprayed insecticide, the BT toxin produced by the plant remains very much there. The BT toxin is known to produce immune responses and allergic reactions. Male rats fed BT corn had a significant increase in three types of blood cells related to the immune system: basophils, lymphocytes and total white cell counts. Sheeps that grazed on BT cotton plants exhibited nasal discharge, mouth lesions, cough, bloating and diarrhoea. The same effects were found in workers who worked on BT cotton farms.

45

Are Soya Protein And Tofu Really As Good As They Are Believed To Be?

Dieters will latch onto any fad. Tofu is one such fad. What is tofu? Tofu can be understood as bean curd. It is made by coagulating soya milk and then pressing the resulting curds into blocks. A lot of claims are made regarding this, such as reducing cholesterol and even helping in post-menopausal flushes. Even otherwise people think very highly of soya bean as a source of protein.

There are many other myths of this type. What people fail to understand is that there are various food items which have nutrients like protein or iron. But the mere quantity of protein or iron does not mean anything. What matters is the quality, which eventually determines how much of it will be absorbed by the body. The 'choona' (slaked lime) which is used in 'paan' is nothing but calcium hydroxide. Does it mean that 'paan' can be used as a calcium supplement? No, because the body cannot absorb calcium in the form of calcium hydroxide. Similarly, though soya bean has considerable amount of protein, the protein is not of good quality. The quality of protein is judged by something called 'biological value', which is based on how much of it can be absorbed by the body. Egg protein has a biological value of 97, cow's milk has a biological value of 90; in comparison soya protein comes at 71 only.

The claims of the health benefits of soya protein made in 1995 are a good example of how research can be subverted. The study was found to be financed by a company called Solae (a division of DuPont), which markets soya products in the USA on a very large scale. The American Heart Association disproved the 'healthy heart' claims in January 2006 after a 10-year-long study. The claims of reducing post-menopausal hot flushes were also refuted. The only benefit of soya protein is that it contains less polyunsaturated fats in comparison to animal proteins. But that is the disadvantage of animal protein and not the advantage of soya protein.

46

Will Eating Cornflakes Improve Your Brainpower?

A certain brand of cornflakes claims that eating cornflakes improves brainpower. In the advertisement there is a child who is dull. After eating the cornflakes he is able to remember even a ten digit number by looking at it just once. Or they show a dull man who is not able to remember anything and others say: *Dimag chalega kaise*? The advertisement claims that cornflakes have iron in them and that makes people intelligent.

This claim is an example of how ridiculous advertising could be and how they could make a fool of the people. Let us examine the claim of iron in it. Even if we accept that it is fortified with iron and vitamins, still what it has got to do with brainpower? They claim that brain needs blood; blood contains iron and hence giving iron would make one more intelligent! Nothing could be more ridiculous. Brain needs the maximum oxygen in human body. It also needs fats, sugar and proteins. Does it mean that eating fats, sugar and protein would make you intelligent, or conversely if your diet is deficient in these? Will making you breathe pure oxygen make you intelligent? There are millions of people who are anaemic; most women become anaemic during pregnancy. Does it mean that they all are stupid or the women become stupid during pregnancy? For that matter, the best dietary source of iron is the liver (kaleji). Does it mean that those who eat liver would be more intelligent? Or if it comes to that, someone can start taking vitamin and iron supplements which are much cheaper than cornflakes. Will he become intelligent after that? There is nothing special about the iron and vitamins in cornflakes. Intelligence is not dependent on diet.

Cornflakes by themselves are not even complete breakfast. The requirements of breakfast vary according to the sort of work one does and what he is going to get in his lunch – those who eat a very light lunch require heavier breakfasts. A 'light' breakfast of cornflakes is not suitable for everybody.

47

Is Drinking Tea Without Milk Any Better Than Drinking Tea With Milk?

Indians traditionally and habitually drink tea with milk. We drink 'chai' which is basically tea boiled along with milk. The British have also been drinking tea with milk. The only difference is that they add milk separately. Chemically it does not make any difference. The Americans are not predominantly tea drinkers; they are coffee drinkers. Their preferred tea is iced tea, which is more of a sherbet. The Russians drink their tea without milk. The Indian leftist comrades copied them, and drinking tea without milk became a style statement. Now drinking tea without milk is considered more happening and intellectual.

There is no evidence that drinking tea without milk has any benefit. The myth had got propagated faster when a German study had reported that arterial blood flow in the forearm was found to be better after drinking tea without milk. Subsequently, the study was criticised on several grounds. Most importantly, it was found that they had studied about 16 subjects only. That is too small a number to draw any meaningful conclusion. Secondly, measuring the blood flow in an artery in the forearm with something as simple as ultrasonogram is no evidence of the overall beneficial effect of something. They had paid no attention to the chemical processes in tea and its digestion.

On the other hand, the fact is that tea contains tannin. Tannins are the compounds used for tanning leathers – hence the name. They bind with the proteins in hides and make them leathery. The addition of milk with tea does the same thing. The protein in milk binds with some of the tannins and makes tea less astringent. Drink tea without milk and also with milk, and you will feel the astringent action on your tongue. Drink tea without milk on an empty stomach and you will realise what it does to your stomach. Drinking tea without milk on an empty stomach causes excessive acidity, which is harmful in the long run as it can lead to stomach ulcers also.

48

Is Organic Food Any Better Than Ordinary Food?

Swearing by the so-called organic food is the latest fashion statement. After all, how do fashionable people distinguish themselves in matters of diet; if they can wear designer clothes, they must eat special food also. Such people have propagated the myth that organic food, which is grown without chemical fertilisers and pesticides and with biotechnology is intrinsically better. The simple fact is that without such things, it is produced less and hence is costlier. Since it is costlier, they believe that it is better. Let us ask the basic questions: Is organic produce safer? Is it more nutritious? Is it friendlier to the environment than conventional agriculture? Is it worth spending more for organically grown food?

There is no scientific basis of such beliefs. A plant has no mind. It does not know whether its nutrition is coming from manure or a pure chemical. The fact is that the plant cannot utilise manure as such. It has to process the manure to produce that chemical which fertilisers give directly. Hence, organic food is not better in any way. In fact, humans too can survive on pure chemicals. But the problem is that we need fibre and above all – taste. Plants do not bother about taste and they are not going to suffer from constipation either. Yes, pesticides are bad when they are used indiscriminately. But if you wash the vegetables properly, most of the residue is removed. Manure, on the other hand, is in fact a breeding ground of all sorts of bacteria, and organic food needs to be cleaned more thoroughly. As for the effect of fertilisers on environment, it is all crap. Abandon fertilisers and you will have billions of starving people because organic farming cannot feed the whole population. We do not mind reverting to ancient ways, but it will be disastrous.

The verdict of the scientists is: "The organic label is a marketing tool. It is not a statement about food safety."

49

Is There Any Nutritive Value In Coca-Cola And Other Soft Drinks?

Hardly anybody needs to be told of the massive sale of soft drinks (carbonated beverages) in this country and abroad. After USA, the most dramatically expanding market of Coca-Cola is India and Mexico. Everybody knows that this is something which sells only on the strength of clever advertising. In this article we are not discussing about the pesticide controversy as it may be a mistake or even irresponsible business practice. Here we are going to show that carbonated beverages are nutritionally useless even if they were to be made to the highest standards.

The carbonated beverages have absolutely nothing in them which can provide any nutrition. In other words, they have empty calories which add to our weight and other health problems. 21 ounces of Coca-Cola give a whopping 210 calories. They come only from sugar and nothing else. In addition, it has 15 mg of sodium which disturbs the sodium balance in the body. You can get this information even on the official website of McDonald's. You will find only zeroes in the column against Coca-Cola. Those children who drink several bottles of Coca-Cola get so many calories from it that they cannot get a balanced diet after that. The high fructose corn syrup used in making it has been linked to obesity and Type-II diabetes. In fact Bill Clinton got Coke dispensers and junk food vending machines removed from the American schools precisely for this reason.

Though the exact formula of Coca-Cola is a very closely guarded secret, certain chemicals have been analysed. The bad effects of caffeine are well known. It also contains phosphoric acid which is bad for teeth. Dr Anthony Starpoli of two New York City hospitals says: "If you look at the components of Coca-Cola, you first see the high acidic content – one of the highest contents of any food or drink. Then you have got the caffeine content, and caffeine will promote acid secretion." Dr Felice Schnoll-Sussman of New York Presbyterian Hospital adds that the upper gastrointestinal tract can only manage so many acidic irritants before reflux trouble begins.

50

Are Antioxidants Really Miraculous Health Supplements?

Articles in popular magazines would have you believe that antioxidants are miraculous food supplements. They are claimed to protect you from ageing, heart disease, strokes, cancer, diabetes, cataracts, arthritis and neurodegenerative disorders such as Parkinson's and Alzheimer's and what not. How did they gain this reputation? Way back in the 1950s it was discovered that something known as 'free radicals' had an adverse effect on health. Free radicals are compounds with unpaired electrons that stabilise themselves by oxidizing other molecules including proteins, carbohydrates, lipids and DNA. In the process they often create more free radicals, sparking off a chain of destruction. Thus they cause what is known as oxidative damage. Then somebody discovered that people whose diets are rich in fruits and vegetables have a lower incidence of heart disease, diabetes, dementia, stroke and certain types of cancer – the very diseases that are associated with free radical damage. Fruits and vegetables are a rich source of antioxidants that can neutralise free radicals by donating electrons to them. Immediately a hypothesis was born that antioxidants were protective and taking them as supplements or in fortified foods should decrease oxidative damage and diminish disease.

Since eating fruits or vegetables was bothersome for the Westerners, the concept helped spawn a colossal supplements industry. The best-known antioxidants are vitamin E (also known by its chemical name tocopherol), vitamin C, and two broad classes of plant chemicals called polyphenols (including flavonoids) and carotenoids (including beta carotene and lycopene). Millions of people take them without bothering whether they work or not.

Scientific research has found that antioxidants work against the free radicals in a test tube, but not inside the human body. When studies were conducted on a large number of people who were given such supplements and then monitored, no effect was found on their chances of getting diseases. The conclusion is clear: whatever is behind the health benefits of a diet rich in fruits and vegetables, you cannot reproduce it by taking their purified extracts or vitamin supplements.

51

Can Certain Food Items Lower Cholesterol Level?

It has become fashionable to talk of food items that can lower cholesterol. Many advertisements on TV and articles in magazines mention things like extra virgin olive oil, oat cereals, nuts like pecans, almonds and walnuts, soya bean, and fish such as salmon, swordfish, tuna and trout. Some food items are described as low in cholesterol whereas some are criticised as high in cholesterol. The impression given in the advertisement is that fibre in some items will clean up your arteries like a broom. This is pure nonsense. What goes in the digestive system cannot enter the blood stream as such.

Cholesterol is one thing about which even doctors have only notions. The American Heart Association has now accepted that most of the notions about the harmful effects of cholesterol are pure myths. Contrary to popular belief, the levels of cholesterol found in the blood have little to do with fats consumed in the diet. Cholesterol is manufactured in the liver in amounts required by the body to perform its various functions such as manufacturing hormones and so on. If your diet has more fat, the liver will produce less cholesterol. Saturated fats have gained an unjust notoriety because they are generally confused with trans fats. Trans fats (unsaturated fats) are harmful because they disrupt cell metabolism.

Cholesterol levels are increased because of a metabolic disorder. It may result in many diseases – heart problem being one of them. The reasons are complex (including genetic and lifestyle) but if we address them, the cholesterol will reduce itself. Thus elevated cholesterol is not the cause of heart disease; it is just a symptom! According to the famous Framingham Heart Study that stretched over 40 years, people above 50 years were found to have no increased overall mortality with either high or low serum cholesterol levels.

Keeping the cholesterol level under control requires a complete change in lifestyle and eating habits – there are no quick-fix solutions to it like eating olive oil or oatmeal.

Part IV

SEX

52

Is Masturbation Harmful In Any Way?

This may perhaps rank as the most highly prevalent myth across the world. Cheap magazines and folklore make young boys and girls believe that masturbation may lead to pimples, poor eyesight, hair on palms and loss of potency or the ability to bear children later in life. It is generally believed by the students that masturbation makes them weak in studies. The most frightful myth is that 40 drops of blood make one drop of semen and hence ejaculation of 1.5 to 5 ml of semen in a single masturbation is equivalent to a loss of 60 to 200 drops of blood, which leads to general weakness. They also suggest that one should store semen for muscular strength in the body. Sportsmen are therefore particularly afraid of masturbation.

The simple scientific fact is that in a normal healthy male, sperms are continuously produced. Those who believe that sperms should be stored in the body never think that there is no place in the body where they could be stored indefinitely and in large quantities. There is very little space for the storage of sperm and it would burst at the end. What they do not know is that like any other cell in the human body, sperms too have a limited lifespan of a couple of days. If sperms are not ejaculated, they die in normal course. The dead sperms are again absorbed in the body and assimilated. If you do not pinch a pimple, the pus would eventually be absorbed in the body. The process with sperms is exactly similar. If one has been ejaculating very frequently, the production rate may not keep pace with it and the number of sperms would be temporarily reduced. That is why it is advised to those males who have difficulty in impregnating that they should abstain for a few days so as to increase the number of sperms.

Muscular strength depends on muscles and the hormone 'testosterone'. Testosterone is not lost by masturbation. Hence masturbation has no effect on strength. There is no evidence of any effect on eyesight, hair growth, etc.

53

Is There Any Particular Food Or Drink That Can Work As Aphrodisiac Or Increase Your Sexual Desire?

Since times immemorial, mankind has been searching for food items or drinks that could increase sexual desire. The search continues even now. Viagra can help sustain a weak erection but it cannot produce sexual desire. It works on blood vessels and not on the brain. Aphrodisiacs are supposed to work on the brain. Throughout the ages, all sorts of strange substances have been claimed to be aphrodisiacs. People poach rhinoceros even now for its horn; tigers are killed even now for their penis soup, which is sold for a very high price in China.

The western world has a long list of food items, which they believe to be aphrodisiacs. There are simple explanations on how food items acquired such reputation. Scientists have explained why they do not work. Oysters, bananas and rhinoceros' horns get into the category because of their phallic shape. Tiger's penis has been included simply because it is the penis of a very strong animal. Testicles of rams qualify for that reason because people think of a he-goat to be sexually attractive. Many food items are considered aphrodisiac because of being soft, silky, smoky, musky, sweet or juicy; all these can be suggestive and alluring. Chocolates came into this category because people believed that women liked them. Some people even discovered that it has a substance called phenethylamine, which has some effect on the brain, though not for sexual excitement. But then it was shown that it is present in a small quantity to have any effect. One of the most notorious of the modern love potions, Spanish Fly is actually quite dangerous. Made from the dried body of a special beetle; it irritates the urinary tract, sending a rush of blood to the genitals. However, it is also a poison, illegal in the United States. Spanish Fly does not create any desire; it only irritates the urethra. Asparagus and artichokes were also claimed as aphrodisiacs. But it was found that their only important ingredients were potassium and folic acid. If somebody has deficiency of these, then they could help with his general health.

There is no genuine aphrodisiac substance discovered yet.

54

Can Drinking Milk On The Wedding Night Help You In Any Way?

This is something that you must have seen hundreds of times in films and TV serials. The bride offers the husband a glass of milk on their first night together. If the persons concerned can afford it, it is kesar-badaam-milk. This has been going on since decades and no one has questioned the idiocy of it. In fact, in some scenes you would actually find the bride herself or the groom's friends exhorting him to drink the milk because 'he would need it'.

The impression, which is sought to be generated by such practices, is that sex on the first night is a highly strenuous activity and the poor groom would not be able to do it unless he is properly fortified with milk. In the first place, the act of intercourse is not a strenuous activity. Did humans not have intercourse for thousands of years when this practice was not developed? The groom is well fed otherwise. He is not a starved man. Then the calories spent in the sexual act stretching to 30-45 minutes come to just about 150. For a starved man, the strength can be obtained by something as simple as a glass of lemonade!

There is no evidence that milk helps in any way to get an erection or keep it for long. Little do they realise that even if milk had some effect, it is not digested immediately! It will take a couple of hours whereas the groom is supposed to proceed for the act immediately after gulping it. Badaam (almonds) takes even longer to digest. Quacks claim that kesar (saffron) helps. But this is pure myth. In India, all things costly are said to have such effects, including a fungi called guchhi (Morel). That is why quacks claim to make *bhasmas* (ash) of gold, pearls and diamond. Saffron contains chemicals like glucocids, protocrocines and picrocrocines. None of them has any such effect and that too in small quantities used in a glass of kesar-badaam-milk. Further, they take too long to digest.

55

Does Size Matter?

The most popular myth about the size of penis is that the bigger the penis the more manly the man and the better he would be able to sexually satisfy a woman.

The length of the penis has little to do with a man's ability to satisfy a woman. The fact is that human vagina is not more than 15 cm (6 inches) long. Irrespective of what they tell you in pornographic websites and literature, the fact is that a penis longer than that cannot go all the way in. Secondly, the vagina does not have nerve endings all along its length, which could support the belief that a longer penis stimulates it better. The vagina has over 90% of its nerve endings only in the first one-third of its length, which is not more than 5 cm. Hence a penis which is only 5 cm (2 inches) long is also adequate for stimulation. There is a solid evolutionary reason for the lack of nerve endings along the whole length of the vagina. If the vagina had nerve endings all along its length, childbirth would have been an excruciatingly painful affair. Even now because of the pressure on the nerves outside the vagina, childbirth is very painful. Nature has struck a balance between sensitivity of a sexual organ and its consequences.

Sexual satisfaction in intercourse depends on many factors. For humans, sex is as much a psychological act as it is biological.

Hence the degree of emotional bonding and intimacy enjoyed are important. Men who think that they can satisfy any woman are mistaken. The other factors, which matter for the satisfaction of the woman, include the degree of arousal, the length of foreplay, the time taken and stimulation of the clitoris and other erogenous zones. As the famous sexologist Dr Prakash Kothari said, "Strength matters and not the length."

56

Is It Possible To Increase The Length And Girth Of Penis By Medicines And Exercise?

A great deal of spam that you receive in your email account pertains to medicines, exercises and special techniques; all of which promise to increase the length and girth of your penis. Why do they send such emails? They know that the size of penis is a matter, which makes most men uncomfortable, and they would rather read quietly about it in the privacy of the email than learn from an authoritative source. Quacks in the countryside sell various oils like that of monitor lizards to increase penis size. Such advertisements capitalise on both the ignorance as well as hidden fears of men.

Exercise can help only muscular tissues. You do bench presses and your pectoral muscles would become bigger. The penis does not have any muscular tissue. The human penis is made up of two types of spongy tissues: corpora cavernosa and corpus spongiosum. During erection, blood is filled in these tissues following dilation of arteries making the tissues increase in size and become stiff. Viagra, for example, is a vasodilator and works by increasing this blood flow. The erectile tissue pinches the veins that carry blood back and maintain the erection. This double function could not have been done by muscular tissue and hence nature did not provide it. Many people go to the extent of hanging weights from the penis. All it can give is some abrasions and cuts, nothing else. Massages with oils of any type also cannot work because oil cannot penetrate the skin and even if it does, it cannot increase the amount of the spongy tissue. Stories of sadhus who could lift bricks with their erect penises are plain lies. Even if they were able to do it, they must have been born with abnormally large penises. No exercise could have made their penises so.

There is no medicine or surgical method that can increase the total quantity of erectile tissue in the penis. A vacuum pump can suck up blood in a flaccid penis and make it erect but it cannot make it longer.

57

Does Breast Size Have Anything To Do With The Sexuality Or Feminineness Of A Woman?

Popular media has placed great emphasis on the size of breasts. Women are as obsessed with the size of breasts as men are with the size of their penises. Many women who do not have large breasts somehow or the other feel inadequate. Otherwise how would you explain the tremendous sales of the padded bras and push-up bras? While perceptions of beauty and attractiveness are subjective, the purpose of this article is to clarify that a woman with small breasts is no less a woman than a woman with large breasts. Misconceptions created by films and magazines are not scientific facts.

The size of the breast is determined by the amount of fatty tissues in it. It has nothing to do with the number of milk-producing glands. Hence breast size has nothing to do with the amount of milk a lactating woman can or will produce. Breast-milk production is stimulated hormonally and increases with demand. Increasing the frequency of breast-feeding sessions with a baby increases the milk supply. Supply meets demand in most cases. While many factors can affect breast-milk production – fatigue, stress and depression – breast size is immaterial.

Researchers have found that breast size does not affect your risk of breast cancer. In addition, it does not affect your treatment outlook. The most common type of breast cancer arises from the cells lining the ducts of the milk-producing glands. Since women with larger breasts do not necessarily have more gland tissue, it makes sense that women with larger breasts do not have a higher risk of cancer.

Finally, the size of the breast has nothing to do with its sensitivity. Hence small breasts do not make any difference to the sex life of a woman. The number of nerve endings in the breast does not depend on its size.

The same things apply to the size of nipples also.

58

Can The Size Of Breasts Be Increased By Applying Creams, Massage Or Exercise?

Most women suffer from the same level of anxiety and fears regarding the size of their breasts as men do regarding the size of their penises. This has led to a huge underground market of methods by which the size of breasts could be increased. Many of such advertisements reach you by spam in your email, whereas some are found aplenty in cheap magazines.

Human breasts are modified sweat glands intended to produce milk. The bulk of the breasts consist of fatty tissue and supporting tissue like collagen and elastin. The fatty tissue gives it the size; the supporting tissue determines its shape. The size of the breast depends on hormonal levels, extent of fat in the body and general health. The breasts have no muscular tissue at all. Rather they sit over the pectoral muscle. Exercise of any type can help only muscular tissue and not the fatty tissue or connecting tissue. Developing the pectoral muscles by exercise is not easy for a woman because she lacks the male hormone 'testosterone'. Some little effect can be expected but it will not have any effect on the cup size of the breasts. The same argument applies to any other massage as well.

As far as the creams are concerned, there is no such substance which can penetrate the skin and influence the metabolism in such a manner that more fatty tissue is deposited in the breasts but not elsewhere. Some of them contain hormones like oestrogen and progesterone – they are wasted as creams. If there is a proven hormonal imbalance, then they must be given internally. Some of them have herbs like fenugreek, fennel, Dong Quai and wild yam in them. They are also wasted as they cannot penetrate the skin and there is no evidence that they can increase the fatty tissue in breasts.

The only proven way of breast enhancement is by surgical implants, though they too have their side effects.

59

Can Anyone Take Viagra And Is It Safe?

Annual sales of the drug Viagra have crossed $ 5 billion in 2007! Honestly speaking, this was the first drug that worked. Hence as soon as it was introduced in 1998, it took the world by storm. The sales figures only show that millions of people are taking it and that too indiscriminately without prescription, particularly in countries like India where getting medicines without prescription is easy. Viagra became popular because it is just a tablet against injections like papaverine hydrochloride that had to be given by doctors in the penis. This meant that people had to go to a doctor, which was very embarrassing. Viagra can be taken quietly on one's own. The question is: Is Viagra completely safe, particularly in view of the fact that people take it themselves? The U.S. Food and Drug Administration has issued warnings about the possible Viagra side effects, and Pfizer is considering changing the warning label.

The drug was initially studied for hypertension and angina pectoris. It works by dilating the arteries, which enables more blood to enter into the penis resulting in better erection. Scientists have warned of the side effects of Viagra due to indiscriminate use. For example, it reacts adversely in those who are taking nitrate-containing drugs such as glyceril trinitrate (nitroglycerin). Viagra is also clearly contraindicated for men suffering from hepatic or renal impairment, low blood pressure, recent stroke or heart attack and hereditary degenerative retinal disorders (including genetic disorders of retinal phosphodiesterases). Since most men do not undergo periodic medical examinations, they could be suffering from one or more of these problems and yet be unaware of them.

A study published in March 2000 found that of the 1,473 adverse drug events reported by the FDA in USA within two years, 564 were caused by the abuse of Viagra. Most of these Viagra deaths were caused by cardiovascular complications. Viagra side effects also warn about temporary vision changes – seeing bluish tinges or having difficulty distinguishing between green and blue.

60

Does Observing Celibacy Make One Stronger And Should Wrestlers Be Celibate?

Presently this is a highly prevalent myth in the country. Thousands of pages have been written exalting the virtues of celibacy or brahmacharya. The popular belief is that indulging in sex makes a man weak because one drop of semen is made up of 40 drops of blood and hence losing 1.5 to 5 ml of semen in one ejaculation makes a man weaker by 60 to 200 drops of blood.

This myth is a classical example of how people forget their own traditions. Some of the strongest men in Indian folklore were not celibates: Bheema, Duryodhana and Balaram ji. They were all happily married men. In the Ramayana, only Hanuman ji is a celibate. And even the Ramayana does not attribute Hanuman ji's strength to his celibacy but to his being the son of Pawan devta and the 'anshavatar' of Bhagwan Shiv. All other characters who were equally strong, such as Jambawanta, Baali, Sugriva, Ravana and Kumbhkarna were married men. Some time down the line, some fool propagated the myth that wrestlers must be celibates.

There is no medical basis of this myth. Today the strongest men of the world are found in the sports of boxing, martial arts, weightlifting, discus throwing, shot put and wrestling. Not even one is a celibate. On the other hand, many of them are known for their promiscuous ways. Modern wrestlers of India do not observe celibacy. But even when wrestlers of the country used to remain celibate, we did not produce a single world champion in any of these sports except Gama! Why do not we produce a celibate man who would beat all those champions by virtue of his celibacy?

Muscular strength depends on how the muscle has been trained. The size of the muscle depends on training as well as hormones – that is why athletes abuse anabolic steroids. There are people who are genetically able to contract their muscles very fast. Bruce Lee's weight was just 59 kg but he could beat heavyweights. None of these factors have any connection with celibacy or sexual activity.

61

Is Indulging In Excessive Sex Harmful?

Indian society has, of late, acquired a very strange attitude towards sex. Many people believe that if they indulge in what they perceive as excessive sex, it would be bad for their health; they would become weak and so on.

The question that haunts most Indians is: how frequently they should have sex, or what the ideal frequency for sex is? For your kind information, most magazines like India Today and Outlook, which publish sex surveys, contain misleading information. The information is collected through dubious means without taking the respondent in confidence. There is no reason to believe that they are telling the truth. Most of the young men who brag about having sex four times a night every day are simply lying because it is considered a sign of manliness if you claim to have sex often.

The point to be noted is that there is nothing called excessive sex or the ideal frequency of sex. The extent to which you can have sex is limited by your desire, physical willingness and your biology. There is no desire, which does not get satiated; there is no human body, which may push itself beyond its biological limits. If the refractory period for a second erection after an ejaculation is, say 20 minutes, you cannot get it in five minutes! You may desire to make love with all the actresses of Bollywood in one night itself but the desire will get satiated after a few. Once the desire is satiated, the body will not respond. In any case, the body will not respond beyond its limits. Within those limits whatever you do, is not going to do any harm. The human body and mind have their own brakes for everything because no system could have evolved with the capacity to self-destruct. Your muscles, for example, cannot generate a force to lift such heavy weights that the spine and the leg bones would get crushed under it; you can generate only as much force as your bones would support. So is for sex.

62

Does Sex In Old Age Do Any Harm?

There is a popular belief that old people should not indulge in sex and if they do, it will be harmful to them. There is no scientific basis for such a belief. It is actually a social expectation. In this country, old people are expected to become bereft of all desire. The moment you retire you are expected to stop even thinking about sex, not to speak of actually doing it. You are regarded as a lecherous old man if you do it. While sex and sexual desire are personal matters and if one decides to abstain from sex even at the age of 50, it is his decision; we must clarify the scientific position.

The scientific explanation is that there is nothing wrong with sex in old age; it does not make you a pervert. A man may marry at 23 and become a grandfather at less than 50 years of age. Should he refrain from sex even at that age simply because social mores expect grandparents to shun sex? If the partners have the desire, then Nature has not decreed that they should not give physical expression to the desire. Many men suffer from erectile problems in old age. In post-menopausal women, hormonal changes make the mucous membrane thinner and more sensitive to pain. Arousal may take a longer time. Hence sex in old age requires longer foreplay for the benefit of both partners so that the man gets a reasonable erection and the woman sufficient lubrication. When intercourse is not possible, sex takes the form of a more diffuse lovemaking in which physical closeness is more important. In fact sex in the old age is more fulfilling as it lays more emphasis on intimacy in relationship than merely a biological act.

Dr Caren Hadders of For Women Only Clinic in Johannesburg says that having sex in old age is more satisfying as there is no fear of pregnancy, the pressures of work and family are less, and the couple has more time to enjoy leisure and intimacy.

Part V

MIRACLES, SUPERNATURAL PHENOMENA AND STUNTS

63

Can Some People Bend Spoons Or Move Objects By Mental Power?

There are people who claimed that by using their mental powers they can bend spoons or move objects. This phenomenon is called psychokinesis. In 1973, an Israeli man called Uri Geller became very famous for allegedly bending spoons and keys. Most people do not even ask as to what is meant by mental power? Power in science refers to the rate at which mechanical work could be done. The mind thinks; thinking is a process inside the brain where electrical signals do the job. The brain cannot move anything by itself because there is no muscle in it. If the brain wants to move something, it sends nerve signals to muscles which do the work. Nerve signals are also electrical impulses. What the brain does, remains inside the brain – it cannot affect anything directly.

The phenomenon of psychokinesis has been thoroughly debunked by James Randi in the USA. He is a magician himself and has shown that all that Geller and other men like him claim to do is nothing but sleight of hand.

A conjuror can create the appearance of a spoon bending while it is gently stroked. Please note that Geller demands to touch the objects for some time. Keep the spoon in a sealed glass jar and do not allow him to touch it; he will not be able to bend it. A momentary misdirection by the conjuror, such as moving around to show the spoon to other people, allows the conjuror to bend the spoon physically. He or she can then disguise the bend with a hand and slowly reveal it at the appropriate moment. When Geller performs the metal bending, he moves the item toward other metallic objects in the room, which he claims enhances the effect. He also frequently fails in his initial attempts to bend the metal but returns to the object a short time later (after trying other psychic effects) and achieves the bend. This again provides the opportunity for misdirection.

Another scientist called Eugene Emery actually photographed Geller in 1987 in the act of bending spoons using his hands.

64

Is Telepathy Possible?

Telepathy means the communication of thoughts between two persons without the help of any spoken, written or other means of communication. In other words, it is a mind-to-mind transfer of thoughts. Telepathy figures greatly in popular writings and films too. Curiously, even those who believe in it have no explanation as to how it could happen.

The biggest doubt on telepathy comes from the fact that no one in the world has been able to demonstrate it. The simple condition is that the people who are demonstrating it should not be known to each other. If they are known to each other then they can collude and cheat. They can decide beforehand as to what they have to say regarding the transferred thoughts. Since there is no end to the range of subjects about which human may think, there are simple ways of checking telepathy. The 'sender' may be shown a randomly selected playing card. The 'receiver' must be kept in an enclosure where he may not receive any sensory input. He then has to tell which card the 'sender' is looking at. There may be some random guesses too but their probability can be discounted. It has been found that no one in the world could ever guess the cards correctly.

Quite often people claim that they get a feeling of a dear one being in trouble. Such claims are not actually the examples of telepathy. If someone dear has gone somewhere and if we are anxious about it, we would be thinking of him only and imagining many things, including the possibility of him being in trouble. If the apprehensions turn true, people tend to attribute it to telepathy. The fact is that in all such cases, we neither get to know the exact nature of trouble (e.g. whether he has met with an accident or has been beaten up), nor do we get to know it at the time when the incident is taking place. Once again no one has been able to demonstrate it.

65

Is There Anything Real About Black Magic?

In this country we have a host of magazines like 'Manohar Kahaniyan', which regularly publish stories about black magic. Bookstalls at railway stations abound in such magazines. What is black magic? How does it differ from stage magic? As far as stage magic is concerned, even if it appears to defy the laws of nature, the fact remains that even magicians admit that it is either sleight of hand or the use of elaborate equipment, which makes the illusion possible. Stage magic is nothing but illusion. There is nothing real in it. The magician who doubles the number of currency notes would not be wasting his time and energy performing the shows had it been really possible for him to double the number of currency notes.

Black magicians are shady characters who operate from frightening places like cremation grounds. It is called black magic because they claim that they can cause harm to others, even death by this. Every year people are murdered in rural areas because people think that if children in their houses are falling sick, it must be because someone has hired a black magician to cast the evil spell.

The philosophy of tantra was not intended to do black magic but there are people who call themselves tantriks and indulge in black magic. The simple fact is that no black magician has ever been able to demonstrate his powers. Had it really been true, every aggrieved person in the country would have been getting his problems solved with the help of some black magician. Politicians too are known for making use of black magicians but nobody has been able to win elections by black magic. There is not a single instance of any man who has been able to win the love of a woman with the help of black magic. People must think that if the magician could really do all that, why does he not accumulate riches for himself and be happy. He cannot argue that taking money would render his skill waste because he does take money for his services.

66

Can Some Sadhus Or Stuntmen Lie On A Bed Of Nails?

This is one of the favourite tricks of Indians. Our sadhus have been performing it since ages. Look up old editions of Ripley's Believe It Or Not and you would find it. It has been shown on Zee TV's programme Shabaash India also.

There is nothing fake about it. It uses a simple principle of physics. If you understand the concept of pressure, it will be clear. Pressure is force per unit area. When you wear flat shoes, you exert less pressure; you wear pencil heels, you exert a high pressure. You see the human skin has certain strength before it ruptures under pressure. If you poke it with a finger, nothing would happen; if you poke with a pin, it would pierce because the area of the pinhead is very small and the pressure is high.

The trick in the bed of nails lies in the large number of nails. Typically they use about 1500 nails. When a man lies on them, his body touches nearly half of them. Thus his weight is distributed over 750 or so of them. This means that for a man of 75 kg, each one of the nails individually gets just about 100 gm of weight. This is not sufficient to pierce the skin. You reduce the number of nails and the pressure exerted by each nail would go on increasing. After a limit, it would become high enough to pierce the skin. Reduce the number of nails and the sadhu would not be able to lie on them.

There is one more cheating involved in it. To show that the nails are real, they drop an apple on it and the nails pierce it. Two things happen here. The apple has a curved surface, which gets into contact with only a couple of nails, which exert a high pressure on it. Secondly, you are dropping the apple from a height, which also adds to the pressure. You place it gently and the nails will not pierce it. Drop the sadhu on the nail bed from a height and see him get pricked.

67

How Do Miracle Workers Get A Heavy Stone Broken On Their Chests?

This is one of the famous tricks shown in India. A very heavy stone is placed on the chest of a miracle worker. It is then hammered with a heavy hammer and the stone breaks. People get amazed at the tremendous strength of the man's chest and he proudly proclaims it to be the result of practicing yoga. The physics of this feat is quite simple. There is no fraud in it – the stone slab is very much real.

The trick lies in the size and weight of the stone slab and the hammer. It has to be a heavy one but not so heavy that it would crush the chest of the man under it. When you hammer it, it amounts to the collision of two bodies of different weights. The energy, which the hammer would deposit in the stone slab, will depend on the ratio of the weights of the two objects. If all other things such as the metal of hammer, its speed and the relative hardness of the metal and the stone, etc. are equal, the maximum transfer of energy too will take place when the weights of the hammer and the stone are equal. But since a man cannot wield a hammer which is as heavy as the stone itself, a clever practical compromise has to be made that would deposit the maximum energy in the stone slab. It so happens that when a sufficiently heavy hammer is struck on a heavy stone slab, it deposits so much energy in the slab that it exceeds the strength of the stone and it breaks.

What will happen if the stone slab is not heavy enough? In that case, a considerable part of the energy will be transmitted to the chest below. Suppose instead of a heavy stone slab, you put just a brick on the chest and use the same hammer. The brick will break surely as it is a weak thing but most of the ribs in the chest would also get broken and the man may very well die.

68

Can Some Yogis Bury Themselves In Pits For Several Days?

In India all of us have heard of yogis who claim that they have such mystical powers acquired by yoga that they can be buried inside a pit for several days and yet come out alive. Many of such yogis demonstrate their miracles at the Kumbh Mela also. The fact is that none of them have ever been able to demonstrate it under foolproof conditions. They do leave some secret hole or even passage for air to come and water to be supplied. Foolproof conditions were tried only once. In October 1980, the so-called Pilot Baba claimed that Khadeshwari Baba would be buried for 10 days in a 10-foot deep pit. Somehow someone really sealed the pit air tight, quite possibly by mistake. After ten days when the pit was opened, they found the decomposed body of Khadeshwari Baba. Pilot Baba went into hiding after that.

Folklore is full of yogis going into Samadhi and remaining there for not days but years. We have all heard that. But in modern times nobody has demonstrated that.

Burial without oxygen defies common sense. The most popular explanation given is that the yogis are able to reduce their vital functions to such low levels that they do not require oxygen. But that does not explain why should they come back after a few days – is there a clock ticking in their system? If they could hold out for ten days, they could as well hold out for ten years. And why do not they demonstrate it in a glass cabin for others to see or at least under a video camera in the pit? It would not be a sacrilege or disturbance either as they do not claim to be doing some secret worship in the pit – they are supposed to enter the Samadhi immediately. And why do they require a pit after all, we could seal their nostrils in the open!

The Pilot Baba was formally challenged by B. Premanand in April 1988 to repeat any of his claimed miracles. He never did.

69

Do Ghosts Really Exist?

Who has not heard of ghosts or met a person who claims to have a ghostly encounter. In fact, the shortest story in the world is a ghost story: In a train someone asked his fellow passenger, "Do you believe in ghosts?" He said, "Yes" and disappeared!

According to believers, a ghost is the spirit of a dead person that either has not moved on to the afterlife or has returned from it. The definition of 'spirit' can vary. Some describe it as a person's soul, while others believe it is an energetic imprint that a person leaves behind in the world. Often ghosts are reported to be the spirits of people who died violently or suddenly; they may re-enact their deaths or try to seek vengeance. (Had that been true, we could dispense with the police and courts, and let the ghosts do justice themselves!) It may be trying to pass a message to friends or loved ones to complete a task that it started while alive, and so on.

Films have added to the imagery. People see apparitions or strange lights, sense a presence in a room, or hear noises. Objects fall from shelves and doors open and close on their own. The electricity goes haywire, causing lights to flicker or televisions to turn on and off by themselves.

In spite of thousands of years of ghost stories, no one has yet been able to demonstrate the existence of ghosts by photographic evidence or otherwise. In UK, Richard Wiseman of the University of Hertfordshire has researched the phenomenon of haunted buildings but nothing could be found to support ghosts. Scientists believe that most cases of ghosts can be explained by hidden fears – if you are afraid in a stormy night in a cemetery, you are likely to see ghosts or hear noises. If you are told that a house is haunted, you will be disturbed in your sleep; if you were not told, you would sleep soundly. Other reasons are simple – people can hallucinate or mistake reflections, shadows or unidentifiable noises for ghosts.

70

Is There Anything Really Mysterious At The Bermuda Triangle?

Most people have heard of the Bermuda Triangle. It is a stretch of the Atlantic Ocean bordered by Florida, Bermuda and Puerto Rico where ships and airplanes are said to mysteriously disappear.

What have made the Bermuda Triangle even more intriguing are the exotic theories. Some say that aliens visit that place and abduct the ships and airplanes; some say that a giant octopus pulls them down to the depths of the sea; one theory says that the lost city of Atlantis was there and that civilisation had many advanced technologies – it is the energy from their crystals and pyramids which does the damage by attacking the navigational instruments of the vessels.

The truth behind the Bermuda Triangle is as follows. Surely, there have been disappearances all right. The US Navy and Coast Guard have done research on the subject. The area is one of the most highly trafficked for amateur pilots and sailors, so more traffic leads to more accidents and disappearances. It is subject to violent and unexpected storms and weather changes. These short but intense storms can build up quickly, dissipate quickly and go undetected by satellite surveillance. Waterspouts that could easily destroy a passing plane or ship are also not uncommon. A waterspout is simply a tornado at sea that pulls water from the ocean surface thousands of feet into the sky. Other possible environmental effects include underwater earthquakes. Scientists have also spotted freak waves up to 100 feet high. Scientists of Cardiff University have discovered the presence of large concentrations of methane gas trapped in the ocean floor. This gas is produced due to the dead and decomposed sea organisms. Within seconds of a methane gas pocket rupturing, the gas surge up and erupts on the surface without warning. If a ship were in the area of the blowout, the water beneath it would suddenly become much less dense. The vessel could sink and the sediment could quickly cover it as it settles onto the sea floor. Even planes flying overhead could catch fire during such a blowout.

71

How Can Some People Walk On Broken Glass?

Some magicians and miracle-workers demonstrate walking on glass. There is no cheating in that. How do they do it? There are no supernatural powers involved in it. There are several ways in which it can be done. There are, however, risks involved and performers at times do get injured.

One of the techniques of walking on broken glass is a pure stunt. In this they use what is known as sugar glass or candy glass. This is what they use in stunt scenes in films when they jump through windows. Broken edges can still be sharp, but the pieces are not usually strong enough to pierce the sole of the foot.

The other technique is to protect your feet instead of using fake glass. One option is to use an adhesive like spirit gum to hold a flexible sole to the bottom of your foot. Another is to use over-the-counter skin-toughening products to make your feet a little sturdier and less sensitive. Many glass walkers use broken wine or champagne bottles. Unlike broken bottlenecks or drinking glasses, these pieces have a relatively gentle curve. You are not very likely to find a piece of glass with multiple sharp edges sticking straight up. The bed of glass is usually kept quite thick.

When you step on it, the pieces shift against each other, moving the edges away from your foot. Some people use a slightly padded surface under the glass, adding a little extra grip. Glass walkers typically take slow steps, repositioning their feet if they get hurt by sharp points. This gives the glass lots of time to settle and adds an extra measure of protection against punctures. Tiny pieces of glass that are likely to embed themselves into the skin naturally sift to the bottom of the pile.

Most importantly, in a glass walk, the weight of your body is spread out over lots of pieces, which have the freedom to move. When you step on a single sliver of glass, your weight is concentrated over that one sharp point and it will definitely get cut.

72

Can Some Strong Men Really Hold Several Cars By Their Arms?

Some time back, in one of the episodes of the programme 'Shabaash India' on Zee TV, one boy of moderate build (and not a 300 pound heavy hulk you see in the WWF shows) was shown holding several cars together. This stunt was very popular in the West earlier where strong men used to show it frequently. It defies common sense. How can they be so strong? The boy held several Maruti vans. A Maruti van has a 37 horsepower engine. Only very strong weightlifters have the power close to even one horsepower. How can a boy have the strength of say ten Maruti vans, equaling 370 horsepower? No way! Then what is the trick?

A very simple principle of physics explains the feat. The secret lies in the way the cars are attached to his body and in the way the cars pull. The cars are tied to his arms by one rope each and form a circle. The man stands in the centre of the circle. All the cars face away from the circle like spokes in a wheel and tries to drive away. What is the catch in the whole thing? The catch is that all the cars pull with exactly the same speed and at the same time. The simple principle of physics says that if something is being pulled in different directions by equal forces as if the forces were spokes on a wheel and if the object were at the hub of the wheel, the net force on the object would be zero. If the cars pull with different speeds or if one of them starts even a fraction of a second earlier or if one of the ropes is slightly shorter, the man would be dragged to the ground in that direction. Further, it is also necessary that the cars pull slowly. If they pull harder or with a jerk, his arms would be wrenched out of their sockets. It is thus nothing but a carefully choreographed event and no feat of superhuman strength.

73

Do Pyramids Possess Miraculous Powers?

It is popularly believed that pyramids have miraculous powers. How this belief originated? Actually, when the ancient pyramids of the Giza Plateau in Egypt first began to be excavated, the mummified corpses entombed within them (along with many of the accompanying artefacts) were discovered to be in remarkably good condition for their age. It was very much evident that the mummies were preserved because of an elaborate process of mummification. In 1973, a man by the name of Patrick Flanagan floated the notion that it was actually because of some mysterious powers of the pyramids that things were preserved in it. Eager to join the bandwagon, some Indians have now started claiming that our ancient sages too knew the powers of pyramid and that the 'Shree Yantra' is actually a pyramid.

Pyramid power is the notion that a regular square-based pyramid, simply by virtue of its shape, can cause miraculous phenomena to occur within its boundaries that would not occur inside other shapes. Flanagan also advanced a fantastic theory that a pyramid acts as a resonator and any electromagnetic frequencies are converted by the direct influence of the perfect pyramid shape causing it to act as an accumulator changing them into a new harmonised form of energy or 'prana'. Of course, he had no answer as to from where this radiation comes and how would it get reflected in a stone pyramid and get converted into 'prana' or vital force which is non-material. The believers claim that razor blades placed inside a pyramid will be sharpened; fruits placed inside a pyramid will stay fresh longer; brain activity will be enhanced by wearing a pyramid-shaped hat. All such myths have been disproved by direct experiment.

Scientists constructed a series of pyramid frames using the precise measurements and dimensions required to 'harness' pyramid power. Four tests were performed: keeping razor blades sharp, preventing food from spoiling (one test for milk, another for an apple) and preventing the decay of a flower. No effect was found at all.

74

How Do Some People Manage To Walk On Burning Coals?

You must have seen it live on TV or seen photograph of the events. Quite a few people are able to walk on burning coals – some do it on special religious occasions, while others do it for show. There is no fraud in it. People do walk on burning coals. How do they do it? Do they have any magical powers? Scientists like David Willey of the University of Pittsburgh have done research on this. He has shown that some basic principles of physics explain this feat. He has pointed out two basic things. The first is the low thermal capacity of coal; the second is the short time for which the firewalker's soles are in contact with the coal.

The people who walk on coals cannot walk on a metal plate which has been heated to exactly the same temperature as the coals. What happens is that coal is made of almost pure carbon. Carbon is a very poor conductor of heat whereas metal is a very good conductor. Stepping on metal would mean that it would transfer heat to the soles very quickly and they would burn immediately. Coal requires a longer time to transfer that heat on contact and the firewalker does not allow that much time to it. Sure they do not run on it, but they do walk briskly. It has been calculated that for a 14 feet walk, the total time for which each foot remains in contact with the coal is about one second only. In any case, no firewalker has ever shown that he could remain standing on the burning coals. There is another catch. The event is always held at night. If it were done during daylight, the bed of coals would look like a bed of ashes. There is always a layer of ash covering the coals. By doing it at night, the glowing red light is still visible through this layer of ash. The ash provides further insulation because it is an excellent insulator. It is used to insulate even iceboxes.

75

How Do Fire-Breathers Show Their Stunts?

Fire-breathing is a spectacular stunt. How they do it? Is there something special about the men who do it? No. The performer directs a mouthful of fuel in a forceful spray over a flame. The result can be a pillar, a plume, or a ball of fire. If it is so simple, what is the catch? Why cannot everyone do it? Above all, the spray must be made with such force that the droplets of fuel that catch fire continue to propel forward in the air even after they have caught fire. Not everyone has that kind of strength in their lungs. The most dreaded risk in fire-breathing is blowback, i.e. the flame following the fuel back to the performer's mouth. One must learn to spew out a whiff of fuel spray and immediately close his mouth.

Then controlling the fuel's direction and the consistency of the spray is a technique that takes a lot of time to refine. Fire-breathers usually practice extensively with water before taking a mouthful of fuel or lighting a torch. They focus on controlling the spray's direction and consistency. Then make sure that they spray it instead of ejecting it in the form of a jet – that requires practice. If the spray is not good enough, the fuel will catch on fire and the fire-breather will fall to the ground and burn. That will spoil the show. Then the angle of spray is also very important. Too high an angle means that the spray can fall on your face itself; too low an angle means it can fall on your body. About 70 degrees is the best.

The choice of the fuel is also critical. It should not be highly inflammable like petrol because any spilling of the spray can result in an accident. It should also not catch fire at too low a temperature as naphtha, alcohol or lighter fluid does. And yet it should produce a brilliant yellow flame. The fuel commonly used is kerosene.

Thus technically speaking there is no fire-breathing. They are actually spewing out fire.

76

What Is Psychic Surgery And Can Miracle Workers Really Operate On A Person With Bare Hands?

Many faith healers across the world claim to have performed psychic surgery. They claim that they can cut the human body with bare hands. Then they proceed to perform the operation (for example, removing a tumor); after the operation, the cut or incision heals by itself. No anesthetic, not much blood either, nothing – not even a scar where the healer had cut.

The whole thing is so outrageous that it has been formally denounced as a total fraud by most countries. Yet magazines keep on writing about it and people continue to believe in it.

It has been shown that the demonstrations of psychic surgery are no better than the sleight of hand used by small-town street magicians who proceed to cut the tongues or other body parts of the subjects on stage. The Federal Trade Commission of USA in fact tried two psychic surgeons and they admitted that the organic matter apparently removed from the patients usually consisted of animal tissue and clotted blood. James Randi, the famous magician who has been debunking all such claims of paranormal, has himself demonstrated psychic surgery. On his

A&E show, the Mindfreak in the episode 'Sucker,' illusionist Criss Angel performed 'Psychic Surgery,' showing first-hand how it may be done (fake blood, plastic bags and chicken livers were used).

Randi says that the healer would slightly roll or pinch the skin over the area to be treated. When his flattened hand reaches under the roll of skin, it looks and feels as if the practitioner is actually entering into the patient's body. The healer would have prepared in advance small pellets or bags of animal entrails which would be palmed in his hand or hidden beneath the table within easy reach. This organ would simulate the 'diseased' tissue that the healer would claim to be removing. If the healer wants to simulate bleeding, he might squeeze a bladder of animal blood or an impregnated sponge. If done properly, this procedure may deceive patients and observers.

77

What Is Faith Healing And Can It Really Work?

Faith healing is big business these days. On several Christian TV channels you will find faith healers like Benny Hinn attracting huge crowds. To put in simple terms, the faith healer claims that he is the intermediary who can invoke God Himself to come to the rescue of a sick person and often heal him miraculously of any problem, however serious it may be. They claim to cure blindness, cancer, polio, tumours, everything. Some times they indulge in outright fraud. People are brought on the stage and they claim that they were suffering from such-and-such disease and that by prayer they have become better. In some other cases they are cured right on the stage. There is no way of finding out whether they are telling a lie. Has anyone ever verified whether they were actually suffering from the said disease as revealed? Even those who are cured on stage are never medically examined on the stage to prove that they are actually suffering from a disease before the miracle nor are they examined after the healing to prove that the condition does not exist anymore. All that you have is the word of the patient. After the miracle, the pastor touches them and they dramatically faint.

Scientists have summarily rejected such gimmicks. Benny Hinn had claimed to cure heavyweight champion boxer Evander Holyfield of a heart condition. Holyfield even presented him with $265,000. Later it was found that a junior doctor had given an incorrect diagnosis from some tests and Holyfield never had any problem. He demanded his money back. In 2002, Joe Nickell of the Skeptical Inquirer wrote a critical analysis of Hinn's healing claims and proved that they were all fraudulent claims.

One of the reasons that people turn to faith healers is that modern medicine has become too impersonal, time-consuming and costly. Most people need some personal attention and assurance, which they do not get in hospitals. Also due to unethical practices of doctors, treatments have become very costly. Hence people look for a short cut.

78

What Is Exorcism And Can People Be Really 'Possessed' By Ghosts?

Right from the remotest villages in India to Hollywood films like 'The Exorcist', we hear of 'possessed' people. Villages in India have had specific temples and *mazaars* which are specialised in exorcism. One of the famous places is Harasu Baram in Bhabhua district, Bihar. The general belief is that evil spirits, demons or ghosts take 'possession' of a person's mind and then the victim starts behaving as the spirit wishes. We already know that there are no ghosts, then why are the so-called 'possessed' people behave in a very strange manner and what happens to them when they are exorcised?

Scientists have repeatedly investigated the matter and they have found that the so-called possessed people are simply suffering from psychological disorders like Tourette syndrome and schizophrenia. Tourette syndrome causes involuntary movements and vocal outbursts; schizophrenia involves auditory and visual hallucinations, paranoia, delusions and sometimes violent behaviour. Psychological issues like low self-esteem and narcissism can cause a person to act out the role of 'possessed person' in order to gain attention. Many sexually frustrated women who become hysteric also exhibit similar symptoms. Under the cover of a hysteric fit they can act out their fantasies.

In the West, exorcism has become big business with exorcism ministries coming up. A particularly popular exorcism ministry in the United States, Bob Larson Ministries, televises its weekly conferences. In these mass exorcisms, large groups of possessed people receive a 'family rate' on tickets. Larson exorcises the demons of an auditorium full of people! You can yourself imagine how ridiculous it is. Once again the fact is that stressed out people want to put the blame of their problems on something else – ghosts or bad Vaastu or whatever.

Exorcism can be dangerous too. In June 2005 in Tanacu, Romania, a 23-year-old nun who lived in a convent was said to be possessed. The exorcists tied her to a cross, stuffed a towel into her mouth and left her alone without food and water. She died. The poor woman had nothing but schizophrenia.

79

Is There Any Basis To Numerology?

The biggest believers of numerology are to be found in the film and television industry where people change the spellings of their names or begin the name of their serials with a particular letter. The fact is that many actresses remain 'C' grade actresses and end up being sexually exploited by every producer in spite of changing their names according to numerology. Many films and serials flop even if their names have been fixed after numerological consultations.

According to numerologists, everything in the world is dependent upon the mystical properties of numbers. Each number has a unique vibration, thus giving it certain properties. These properties can shed light onto a person's behaviour or predict whether their romantic partners are compatible. Numerological analysis can determine a person's lucky number or lucky day. In fact some people report the recurrence of a number in their lives.

Have you ever asked yourself how could numbers have vibrations? Only real things can vibrate. Numbers are abstract things. How can a number vibrate? Can there be anything more ridiculous? Scientists have disproved numerology from various angles. The recurrence of some numbers is purely coincidental. Because of the limited number of numerals that exist in the world, repetitions are inevitable. The fact is that people are good at recognizing patterns. While this helps people to read, count and recognise faces, it also encourages people to interpret random events as patterns.

Thus people are likely to remember seeing their numbers and forget seeing other numbers. In other words, a person whose number is seven will remember seeing lots of sevens while disregarding all the sixes, eights and other numbers he encounters.

Finally, the biggest fraud of numerology is that it is based on an invented system of counting. The decimal system developed allows people to count objects in groups of ten, mostly because people have ten fingers on which they count. Computers use a binary system with only two digits, 0 and 1 for everything. The patterns would not be found in any other system.

80

Do Vampires Really Exist?

Who has not heard of Dracula? In fact vampires have been a part of folklore much before Dracula came into existence. People have been dreaming of horrible monsters and malicious spirits for centuries. According to the predominant mythology, every vampire was once a human, who after being bitten by a vampire, died and rose from the grave as a monster. Vampires crave the blood of the living, which they hunt during the night. They use their protruding fangs to puncture their victims' necks. A vampire may also take the form of an animal, usually a bat or wolf, in order to sneak up on a victim. The legend is that vampires do not cast a reflection and they have superhuman strength. It is also believed that they can be destroyed by a stake through the heart, fire, beheading and direct sunlight, and they are wary of crucifixes, holy water and garlic.

Needless to say, there cannot be anything like a vampire. No real vampire has ever been found. A dead person cannot come back to life. If at all a person has been found to be sucking blood, he has to be a living person. There are a number of real medical conditions that might result in vampire-like behaviour or appearance. Psychologically, people suffering from disorders like schizophrenia could exhibit strange behaviour. Physiologically, porphyria is a rare disease characterised by irregularities in production of heme, an iron-rich pigment in blood. People with more severe forms of porphyria are highly sensitive to sunlight, and experience severe abdominal pain and may suffer from acute delirium. One possible treatment for porphyria in the past might have been to drink blood to correct the imbalance in the body (though there is no clear evidence of this).

The root cause of the vampire lore is nothing but fear. The appearance of so many vampire-like monsters throughout history as well as our continued fascination with vampires, demonstrates that this is a universal response to the human condition. It is simply human nature to cast our fears as monsters.

81

Can Black Magic Or Some Other Trick Bring Back The Dead And Make Them Zombies?

Horror films of Hollywood and horror serials back home in India frequently show stories of black magicians or similar persons who convert the dead persons into zombies. A zombie is a dead person who has been brought back to life by black magic and then he becomes a mindless slave to the magician, bereft of any willpower at all. All he knows is to obey his master's commands. The zombies do not feel any pain, hunger or thirst. At the command of the magicians they would continue to fight even after they have lost their limbs. Obviously, having such persons gave immense power to the magician – hence the fear.

There are several possible origins for the word 'zombie.' These include jumbie, the West Indian term for 'ghost,' and nzambi, the Kongo word meaning 'spirit of a dead person.' The zombie folklore originated in Haiti. Black magicians practicing voodoo are supposed to have made zombies.

In 1980, a man appeared in a rural Haitian village. He claimed to be Clairvius Narcisse, who had died in Albert Schweitzer Hospital in Deschapelles, Haiti 18 years ago in 1962!

Narcisse described being conscious but paralysed during his presumed death – he had even seen the doctor cover his face with a sheet. Narcisse claimed that a magician had resurrected him and made him a zombie. One Dr Wade Davis investigated the matter. He suspected that some sorcerers were secretly administering the puffer fish poison tetrodotoxin to their victims. It produces paralysis and a near death-like condition but the effect eventually wears off. The sorcerer could steal the person if his relatives gave him up for dead and wait for him to become normal. Though the theory appeared interesting, it could not explain how the zombie subsequently lose his mental faculties and become slave-like – a victim of poisoning should have become normal after recovery. Now scientists believe that if a person exhibits zombie-like behaviour, he must be a physically normal living person but he must necessarily be suffering from a serious mental disorder and mistaken identity.

82

What Are Séances Or Planchettes And Can You Talk To The Spirits Through Such Things?

This is the bread and butter of horror films and serials. In a séance (French for 'session'), a frightening looking woman or man acts as the medium. This person goes into a trance and the spirit comes on him. Then the spirit or ghost communicates its message through the medium. Some times the medium starts speaking in a strange voice, which is interpreted as the spirit speaking through him. At times a pencil in his hand starts writing messages. A planchette (French for 'small table') is nothing but a small board on which the pencil moves. They were very popular in 19th century Europe.

Many people believe that spirits either wander or wait in heaven from where they can be summoned. Mediums, séances and planchettes exploit the anxieties of people amongst such believers who are deeply troubled by deaths and cannot reconcile to the fact. Some of them have guilty consciences and they want to expiate by 'talking' to the spirits.

The believers of this nonsense were never able to answer some basic questions – Who becomes a ghost or spirit and who does not? Which spirit comes over the medium and which does not? Who can become a medium and who cannot? If the spirits are so powerful that they can take control of a living body, why do they need the medium at all? Are they good enough only to cry for their grievances and unfinished work? If they can make the medium speak in their voice, they should be able to do other things also, such as take revenge, complete unfinished work by taking control of just anybody. Why should we not use them to reveal secrets known only to them?

Ray Hyman has shown in his study in 1999 (The Mischief-Making of Ideomotor Action) that mediums are fraud. The writing by the pencil is attributed to what is known as the ideomotor effect wherein a subject makes motions unconsciously (i.e. without conscious awareness). As in reflexive responses to pain, the body sometimes reacts reflexively to ideas alone without the person consciously deciding to take action.

83

How Do Some Religiously Devout People Burn Camphor On Their Hands Or Tongues?

This is a staple of devotional films. Many people do it in real lives also. The hero or the heroine walks around the temple with camphor burning in his or her hand. At times they would worship with the camphor burning in open palm. In more daring shows, some people place it on their tongues as well. How do they do it? There is nothing fake in it. It is done for real. What is the explanation then?

It is a matter of simple physics. Camphor has two properties. It is highly inflammable. It is also a good insulator of heat. So what happens when you burn a block of camphor? It burns from the top. Yet because, it is also an insulator, it does not transmit the heat below. The block of camphor acts as the insulator between the flame and the bottom of the block. Hence if you place the block on your hand and burn it, your palm will not feel much heat. However, if the block is very thin, it will transmit heat. Hence the trick lies in keeping a sufficiently thick block of camphor. You can place it on your tongue also. But you will have to extinguish it before it becomes thin enough to cause burn.

Performers do not let the block burn to the finish in the first place. Secondly, they calculate the correct thickness of the block.

The trick can also be repeated with any substance, which has similar properties. In fact there is a high explosive substance called guncotton. It is made by treating ordinary cotton with concentrated nitric acid. It is an explosive in a compressed form but merely burns when it is loose. If you take a quantity of guncotton in loose form and place it on your hand to burn it, it will burn so fast that you will not feel any heat on your palm. In fact at one point of time this was used as a test to find out whether the guncotton has been properly made or not.

84

How Do Some People sSwallow Swords?

Sword swallowing is almost as old as human civilisation. Ancient Romans also did it. Of late it has been shown on Zee TV's programme Shabaash India. There is nothing false about swords being swallowed nor is there anything magical in it. The trick is that the sword blade must be a very flexible one. There is no way a stiff blade can be swallowed. Even with a flexible and thin blade there is considerable risk involved. The basic mechanism is rather simple. As the sword goes through the gullet, it should move only along the length. The performer does it in such a controlled manner that there is no sideway movement of the blade at all. Hence it does not cut. This requires years of practice and that is why not everyone can do it. He should also be able to judge very accurately as to when he should stop. The sword point should not touch the stomach!

Those who practice it must first overcome their gag reflex at objects touching the back part of their mouths. Long practice controls this reflex. The pharynx must also be conditioned. Objects introduced here cause much pain, and only after several trials can they be passed without great discomfort. The stomach is conditioned in a similar manner.

More importantly, in psychological terms, it takes years of practice and a strong mind-over-matter mental attitude to consciously relax one's mind and body, repress the gag reflex and wretch reflex, get past the uncomfortable sensations, focus very carefully on the correct alignment and placement, making sure you are directing the blade exactly where it needs to go without puncturing yourself. Combining these physical and mental disciplines correctly every time is what makes sword swallowing so extremely difficult and dangerous. There is always the risk of damage to the throat, vocal cords, oesophagus, lungs or stomach, and if it should happen – a lacerated or perforated oesophagus or punctured stomach – will be very difficult to treat and prove fatal at times.

85

Can Some People Really Chew Glass And Swallow It?

This is one of the oldest folklores of India. Recently someone demonstrated it on Zee TV's programme Shabaash India also. Paul Brunton, a British traveller, has also mentioned it in his book *A Search in Secret India* about one such man in Calcutta. The general claim was that the miracle worker had some mysterious yogic powers by which he could digest glass and even poisons. Most people remember only that. What they do not know is that the same Paul Brunton has mentioned later in the book that after one performance in Dacca, the miracle worker actually died after consuming poison – his claimed yogic powers could not save him. Glass pieces, swallowed as such, would cut the stomach badly. How do they do it then?

There are two ways in which this trick is performed. One is the usual filmy trick. The glass used is the so-called sugar glass. It is the glass that is used in windows through which heroes jump without getting even a scratch. It is nothing but sugar candy and gets dissolved in stomach.

The other technique is real but far riskier. This technique has been demonstrated by B. Premanand, Convenor, Indian Committee for Scientific Investigation of Claims of the

Paranormal, Podanur, Tamil Nadu. In 1989 he demonstrated it in Delaware, USA. He took a light bulb. It was verified by Larry Weinstein that it was not a clear candy. Weinstein then placed the chip on Premanand's tongue. Premanand chewed it well and then swallowed a glass of water. He poured it into his mouth from a distance to show that he was not simply spitting the unchewed glass into the water.

He himself explained that if one chews a glass, one must chew it very finely into a powder. Then make sure that one has eaten something thick and viscous like bananas or mashed potatoes just before, so that the glass powder does not settle alone in the stomach and gets wrapped in the banana or potato mash. The technique, even then, is fraught with risks.

86

Do Some Animals Have A Sixth Sense By Which They Can Predict Death?

You must have heard in your childhood that it is a bad omen if a dog is found crying in the neighbourhood because it meant that someone will die shortly. Interestingly, the myth has been carried further. In July 2007, it was reported that a cat could 'predict' the deaths of patients in a nursing home several hours before they died. Oscar, a cat adopted by the staff of the Steere House Nursing and Rehabilitation Center in Providence, Rhode Island, USA was claimed to have at least 25 successful predictions. He is said to sniff and watch the patient before sitting down near him. He would leave soon after the patient had died.

Scientists investigated the matter. Most scientists believe that the phenomenon is as simple as Oscar enjoying the comfort of electrically heated blankets placed over the dying patients and leaving when the heat is switched off. They have pointed out that the behaviour of Oscar in keeping vigil next to dying patients is also explained by its mimicking the behaviour of the staff of the hospital. After all, Oscar has almost become a domesticated cat and they do copy behaviours of human companions. Some people speculated that the cat could be drawn to specific smells produced by the dying patients. That is, people who are dying emit certain chemicals that are not detectable by humans but that may pique Oscar's heightened sense of smell. Surely, animals can detect smells, which humans cannot and that includes smells related to death also. Animals can sense sickness in their human and animal friends by smells or noticing changes in their behaviour, such as someone lying down at odd hours. Animals do become very disturbed also if someone close to them dies. Dogs have cried for days when their companions have died – many dogs have died of grief following the deaths of their masters. But that does not mean that animals have something built into them which will make them compulsively drawn towards the smell of death, seek out dying people and sit next to sick people by way of announcing impending death.

87

Are The So-Called Out-Of-Body Experiences (OBE) Claimed By Some People Real?

This myth has become quite popular in the west these days. In an out-of-body experience, a person claims to have seen his body from a vantage point outside his physical self. Yoga philosophy does not find anything unnatural in it. They have always believed in the atma (soul) as distinct from the physical body and it is only the great yogis' atma, which can leave the body at will and then come back, as Adi Shankaracharya was claimed to have done. For the rest, the atma leaves the body only when the body dies. Thus out-of-body experience (OBE) in Yoga philosophy is an exception and there is no modern evidence for that. The westerners believe in OBE without even believing in the existence of the atma.

Scientists have found that the claims of the so-called OBE are usually associated with serious illness, accidents, seizures, near-death experiences or other traumatic events. They are actually hallucinations. They result from a lack of oxygen that alters brain activity, and acute stress to which the person is subjected.

Those who believe in the OBE have never been able to explain as to what is it that comes out of the body and then views it as if it were completely detached to it. It cannot be the brain for the brain is a part of the body. The problem is that if they accept the existence of the atma then they will have to believe in the transmigration of souls also. That would run counter to their religious beliefs; in Christianity the soul does not take rebirth but waits for the Day of Judgement. The fact is that they want to believe in something mystical just for the heck of it.

British researchers at the University College London Institute of Neurology and Swiss researchers at the Laboratory of Cognitive Neuroscience at the Ecole Polytechnique Federale conducted experiments, which proved that the brain could indeed be tricked. In one experiment a subject was tricked into thinking that a rubber hand was his real hand.

88

Is There Really Anything Called ESP (Extra-Sensory Perception)?

In your life you must have certainly met some relative or friend who would have claimed that he had a premonition of the death of somebody close to him or that he had a dream that someone close had died at some other place and it turned out to be correct. People claim to get dreams which tell many important things that subsequently do take place. Some people claim that somehow they get a knowledge of something that is happening at a remote place. All such things are collectively known as ESP (extra-sensory perception).

All the so-called evidence in support of ESP is only anecdotal. No one in the world has ever been able to demonstrate any ESP whatsoever. Dr Abraham Kovoor of Sri Lanka had declared a reward of Rs one lakh decades ago with a challenge to show it, but nobody could ever do it. Now James Randi in USA has offered a reward of a million dollars for any successful demonstration. Several high-profile professed psychics have accepted the challenge and then backed out, which in itself is enough to bust them. During the years of the Cold War, the CIA did research on self-proclaimed psychics to find out if they could tell the locations of the Soviet nuclear submarines in the oceans by looking at the photograph of the commanders or the submarines. Millions of dollars were spent to reveal the secret, but they could never tell anything.

The claimed instances of ESP are purely statistical chances. To the average person, a dream or feeling coming true in precise detail seems too amazing to be simple coincidence. But if you look at it from a statistician's viewpoint, it is much less incredible. There are more than 6 billion people on earth, constantly thinking and experiencing dozens of significant events every day. Statistically, on any particular day, some of the things people envision will line up closely with some of the things those people happen to experience. The chances of a 'hit' climb even higher when you consider people's ability to make reasoned, educated guesses.

Part VI

GENERAL SCIENCE

89

Can Mobile Phones Cause Cancer?

Many people believe that the radiation from mobile phones can cause cancer. Half-baked articles in popular magazines and in the electronic media have propagated this myth. There is very good scientific evidence that using mobile phones does not increase your risk of any type of cancer. Many research studies in Europe and the US have failed to find an increased brain cancer risk due to mobiles. And most of the researches have been done on older analogue phones. Modern digital phones give out even less radiation. In a massive Danish study conducted for 420,095 mobile phone users, they examined the cancer rates of cell phone users who began using cell phone from 1982 to 1995 and followed their cancer rates through 2002. Denmark was an ideal place for this study because they keep a national cancer registry. This is a system that logs and tracks every person who is inflicted with the deadly disease. In the research study, cancer appeared in only 14,249 people, as opposed to 15,001 cases that appeared in the general population. Thus it was established that cell phone users had no higher risk of brain tumours, acoustic neuromas, salivary gland tumour, eye tumour, or leukaemia.

There is a good logic for believing in the study. Cancer can be caused if the radiation damages the DNA of your cells. It is true that mobile phones transmit and receive microwave radiation, but this radiation does not have enough energy to damage the DNA, and cannot directly cause cancer. The energy of the microwave radiation used in the mobile phones is millions of times lower than the energy contained in the X-rays used for diagnostic purposes which you take fearlessly.

So far, the only proven health issue associated with mobile phones is an increased risk of car accidents! People who use mobile phones while driving, even with a hands-free kit, are easily distracted and are four times more likely to be involved in an accident.

90

Does Alternating Current Pull You Towards The Source?

One of the myths regarding electric shocks is that if you get electric shock from alternating current, you will get stuck to the wire and would not be able to pull yourself away. You must know how electricity affects human body.

Electricity has two components, namely voltage and current. Current is more important. There are many devices that produce high voltage, such as spark plugs of cars or even the gas lighter, which you use in kitchen for lighting the gas, but their current is very low. Hence they do not do any damage. Domestic supply, on the other hand, has only 220 volts but the current is quite high – up to 30 amperes. Hence it can be lethal.

In direct current (dc), the polarity is always constant. The positive of a battery remains positive. Alternating current (ac) means that the polarity of a wire keeps on changing; a point, which was positive, will become negative after a short time and so on. Domestic supply changes polarity 50 times in a second. It is a known fact that current flows from positive to negative. When you get shock from a dc supply, the current flows only in one direction. When you get shock from an ac source, the current flow changes direction 50 times a second. Current flow through the muscles and makes them contract. Alternating current makes the muscles contract repeatedly with its frequency. You will literally feel them vibrating at the rate of 50 times per second. If the time of contact happens to be large and since human muscles are not designed to contract so rapidly, it may throw them into a spasm. Then you feel as if you have lost control over your muscles. It is this spasm that makes one feel as if he is stuck to the source. The current by itself does not exert any pull on you. For the same voltage, you would be able to pull your hand away from a dc shock if the current is 75 milliamperes; with ac it would need only 15 milliamperes.

91

Is A Detergent Powder That Produces More Foam Better Than A Detergent Which Produces Less Foam?

Indians believe that a detergent giving more foam is better. Detergent-making companies have thrived on this myth for long. Remember the Nirma jingle: *Thoda sa powder aur jhaag dher saara?* Or '*Deepikaji, magar aap to wo mehengi wali titkiya…*', which is answered with '*wahi safedi wahi jhaag, jab kam daam mein mile to koi woh kyun le, yeh na le?*' Unfortunately it is not true.

Soap cleans by acting as an emulsifier. Basically, soap allows oil and water to mix so that the oily grime can be removed during rinsing. Detergents are primarily surfactants. Surfactants lower the surface tension of water, essentially making it 'wetter' so that it is less likely to stick to itself and more likely to interact with oil and grease. Cleaning products may also contain enzymes to degrade protein-based stains, bleaches to de-colour stains and add power to cleaning agents, and blue dyes to counter yellowing. Detergents are similar to soaps, but they are better in the sense that they are less likely to form films (soap scum) and are not as affected by the presence of minerals in water (hard water).

Neither detergents nor soaps accomplish anything except binding to the soil until some mechanical energy or agitation is added into the equation. Swishing the soapy water around allows the soap or detergent to pull the grime away from clothes or dishes and into the larger pool of rinse water. Rinsing washes the detergent and soil away. Warm or hot water melts fats and oils, so it is easier for the soap or detergent to dissolve the soil and pull it away into the rinse water.

Now you can see that there is nothing in the action of detergents that makes the foam of any consequence. In fact foam can create problems in washing machines. If the detergent foams unduly, the foam overflows onto the floor and can also interfere with the free flow of clothes through the water. In automatic machines the foam can interfere with water level pumps and the proper working of the control in machine.

92

Does Cigarette Smoking Help In Concentration?

Smokers have many excuses for smoking. The most popular of them is that smoking helps them concentrate. It means the smokers smoke when they have to do something that requires intense concentration. It is also claimed that smoking helps the mood and is helpful when depressed.

This excuse does not have any medical proof but is just a fake explanation that provides the smokers with a chance to continue their cigarette smoking.

Every habitual person who is in the process of getting rid of smoking has to face withdrawal symptoms. At times, the person becomes annoying and restless. He takes these symptoms as a negative effect and again wants to have a puff to feel relieved. Nicotine in cigarette makes the smoker feel at ease. For a short time nicotine intoxicates and relaxes the mind. Hence one feels relaxed temporarily. It has nothing to do with concentration. Further, since nicotine is addictive, the dependence on nicotine goes on increasing. That is to say, one gets more relaxation if he smokes a cigarette after undergoing a period of anxiety and restlessness. Since an annoyed, anxious or restless man cannot concentrate whereas a relaxed man can, he misinterprets the result as improvement in concentration.

The myth of better concentration is an outcome of psychological perceptions of most of the smokers. The fact is that cigarette smoking lessens the concentration power instead of improving it. One of the effects of nicotine is that the arteries get blocked and supply of oxygen to the brain is decreased due to which the person lacks in concentration. French researchers, Pier-Vincenzo Piazza and Djoher Nora Abrous, at the National Institute for Health and Medical Research have found that nicotine has adverse effect on the intellectual capacity also. Nicotine causes a fall in the protein PSA-NCAM. This protein plays a vital part in the adaptability of the brain and is related to an ability to learn and memorise. You can see the effect for yourself.

93

Does Drinking Alcohol Or Eating Chicken Help You Cope Better With Cold Weather?

A very popular myth pertaining to winters is that one must either drink alcohol or eat chicken or nuts like almonds to cope with it. Winters become an excuse for drinking alcohol as it is supposed to keep one warm. People say that eating tandoori chicken and drinking a quarter of whisky will not affect you in the cold weather. Vegetarians swear by nuts – the common belief is that nuts like almonds, walnuts, etc. must be eaten.

There is no scientific basis of such beliefs. Dr William G. Haynes, Director of Clinical Pharmacology at the University of Iowa College of Medicine has found that alcohol may make you feel flushed. The skin may also feel warm because it dilates the blood vessels. Both these effects have nothing to do with any heat generation in the body or your ability to withstand cold. The flow of blood to skin actually reduces the core temperature of the body. Alcohol has a high affinity for water. As you drink alcohol, it passes from the gullet to the stomach and draws water from the wall lining. It is this action, which produces the characteristic burning sensation. There is no heat generated at all. Full digestion of alcohol is a long process. It first gets converted to acetaldehyde, which then gets converted to acetic acid and finally acetic acid gets converted to carbon dioxide and water. The calories from alcohol get accumulated after several hours and they are empty calories without any nutrition. Similarly chicken and nuts, which are high calorie food, also require several hours to digest. Nutritionally they are better than alcohol in the sense that they do not give empty calories, but it does not mean that if you eat chicken or almonds, you can immediately walk shirtless in cold weather.

Research on men who undertook arctic expeditions has shown that there are no particular nutritional requirements specific to long-term operations in the cold other than the requirement for sufficient energy consumption to balance energy expenditure.

94

Does A Large Head Or Large Forehead Mean That The Person Would Be More Intelligent?

It is widely believed that if a person has a large head or forehead then he would be more intelligent. A considerable amount of racism has been perpetrated on this belief. The simplistic argument which they gave was that a large skull meant that there was more brain matter, and more brain matter meant that there was more intellectual capacity. During the ancient times in India, it was believed that Brahmins had large heads and foreheads. In the western world, men like Samuel Morton went onto write books in the 19th century to show that the average Caucasian skull was bigger than the average Negroid skull.

Modern science has disproved it completely. There is no relation of intellectual capacity with the size of the skull and the amount of brain matter. Even bodily strength does not depend only on the size of the muscle. It also depends critically on how it has been trained, how many fast twitch fibres it has, and so on. Had it been true, the largest men would have been the strongest. It is not so. Many champion weightlifters are not the largest men in their weight category.

The same thing applies to brain also. Memory in the brain is not like the hard disk of a computer, which has fixed storage space, and you cannot exceed that. Intelligence is not like the RAM of a computer that a 2 GB RAM would make your computer faster. The number of neurons keeps on falling continuously after adolescence. Does it mean that we become less intelligent as we age? In fact many people become intellectually better with age. The functioning of the brain is very complex and neurons work in a collective manner. It is not that you remove one neuron and the information stored therein would be lost – other neurons simply take over its task. Like muscles, intellect largely depends on how you train the brain, how much information you put in it. Some of the geniuses in history did not have large skulls.

95

Can Hypnotists Really Take Complete Control Of Your Mind?

Mention the word hypnosis and the first thing that would come to your mind is Mandrake, the magician. Most of us have read Mandrake comics in our childhood. The common theme is that Mandrake gestures hypnotically and the man in front starts seeing things which Mandrake wants him to see. That has really distorted the perceptions of many people.

What is hypnosis after all? Does it mean that you lose all your conscious control under hypnosis? Does it mean that you become a mere puppet in the hands of the hypnotist and you would even commit a murder if he asked you to do so, and afterwards you would not remember anything at all? Does it mean that the hypnotist can pry into the deepest secrets of your mind? All such notions are false. Had there been any truth in them, hypnotists would have been the most powerful people on earth. But it is not so.

Hypnosis is 'a trancelike state that resembles sleep but is induced by a person whose suggestions are readily accepted by the subject.' This means that you have to be willing to be hypnotised. You have to consciously accept the suggestions of the hypnotist. You cannot be hypnotised against your will. In fact you can hypnotise yourself too and it is known as self-hypnosis. Hypnosis is a matter of suggestions and the stories of hypnotists swinging a crystal before your eyes or asking you to look at a flame are false. The stage performances of hypnosis are stage-managed dramas.

Hypnosis has limited medical uses in treating anxieties and phobias, depression, smoking habit and pain in some small surgical procedures like dental procedures or biopsies. It cannot do anything more than that. You cannot expect that an operation of appendicitis can be done under hypnosis without anaesthesia.

A man under hypnosis does not lose all his control. He will not do anything, which is against his basic instincts. You ask a woman to take off her clothes and her trance will break immediately.

96

Are The So-Called Acupressure Seats In Cars Of Any Use At All?

You would find acupressure seats everywhere. They are actually nothing more than a mat made of wooden or even plastic beads. Generally they are draped over the seat of the car. Some are placed on the bottom also. The claim is that the beads press your acupressure points and thus save you from backache or tiredness after a long drive.

The fact is that they are perfectly useless. In the first place, the efficacy of acupressure itself is doubtful. Secondly, even if you believe that acupressure works, the so-called acupressure seats defy the basic principles of acupressure. Acupressure says that there are certain specific points on the surface of the body, which are 'somehow mysteriously connected' to certain internal organs. If you apply pressure on those points, it would affect those organs. Nobody knows how it would happen and why it should happen in the first place. It has never been demonstrated successfully in controlled clinical trials. Such systems were developed in ancient societies when even rudimentary medical systems were not developed.

Secondly, the so-called acupressure seats have their beads (that supposedly exerts pressure) uniformly distributed. That goes against the very concept of acupressure because those beads are uniformly exerting pressure on numerous points on the body and not on specific points as required by acupressure. Some desirable acupressure points might get accidentally pressed in the process but the pressing of an equal number or more of undesirable points would negate the effect. If anybody claims any positive effect of these seats, the effect is purely psychological.

Thirdly, the seats make the bottom or the back slippery. Having a slippery bottom is not advisable for the driver as it may affect his driving position and result in his body shifting from a comfortable position every time he brakes or accelerates.

97

Is Time Travel Possible: Can One Visit The Past Or The Future?

Most people are thrilled by the idea of time travel. This is the biggest fantasy of mankind ever since H. G. Wells wrote the *Time Machine*. Science fiction films and novels would have you believe that time travel is possible. But is it really possible to travel in the past or the future? People think that if they could go to the past, they could meet their departed ones or witness historic moments. Many others want to go to the future and come back so that they may suitably alter it.

By common sense it should not be possible. However, people are misled when occasionally publicity-hungry scientists also float such views in the media. Such scientists only speak of a mathematical possibility. For example, if the equations say that negative time is also valid, such people would conclude that travel to the past is possible.

Some others have been fiddling with very high-level theories of astrophysics. It was suggested that one could travel in time through wormholes. It is a hypothetical tunnel connecting two regions of space-time. The regions bridged could be two completely different universes or two parts of one universe. Matter could theoretically travel through either mouth of the wormhole to reach a destination on the other side. Other scientists have, however, pointed out that to punch a hole in the fabric of space-time it would require energy as high as that of a star. How could humans ever produce that sort of energy?

All such people do not realise some basic things. What would happen if, in the course of your time travel, you interfere with the happenings of the past or future? If someone really travelled to the past and killed his own ancestor before he had kids, how would he ever be born in the first place? Similarly, if one could come back from the future and do something that would alter the future, it would mean that the future that he had visited was not real?

Time travel is therefore not possible.

98

Do Flying Saucers Or UFOs Really Come To The Earth?

The popular belief is that there are highly advanced civilisations somewhere in the universe, which come to us in flying saucers to investigate us. Some have reported that people were actually kidnapped by the aliens so that they could study them the way biology students study frogs.

Numerous scientific bodies have examined all the cases of UFO sightings. They are all convinced that people have mistaken weather balloons, relatively unknown military aircrafts or even natural phenomenon like ball lightning for UFOs.

There are, however, some very simple to understand reasons as to why there cannot be flying saucers. Even if we accept that there are aliens on other planets, let us first look at how far they are. Though several planets have been discovered in the solar system, there is no evidence that they are in a condition to support life. One of the planets found nearest to us is orbiting the star Upsilon Andromedae. It is 44 light years away from us and if a spaceship were travelling at the speed of light (for nothing can travel faster than that); it would require 88 years for a round trip. Is it practical? Then let us look at it this way. A civilisation that can make spacecrafts travel at the speed of light, does it really need to come to the earth physically to learn about us? They would be ahead of us in technology by millions of year – can't they find about us sitting right there?

All reports say that flying saucers fly incredibly fast. Then why don't they make noise? You swing even a stone on a string and it will make noise. Everyone knows the noise which aircrafts make. How come nobody has reported about any noise from a flying saucer? It can only happen if they were balloons or ball lightning. And then why should their spaceships be like flying saucers? The reason is that people know that a rocket shaped like our rockets cannot reach the stars. Hence they imagined a different shape.

99

Is Yawning Contagious?

Do you feel like yawning if somebody near you is yawning? Some people believe in it; some dismiss it as a myth. So far it is not exactly known as to why do humans and animals yawn. The most commonly believed theory is that we yawn when we are tired. The level of carbon dioxide in the blood rises and the body needs more oxygen. But we also yawn when we are bored. You can see many students yawning during a boring lecture. By yawning we also express emotions like apathy, apprehension or remorse. It has also been theorised that yawning is a means of cooling the brain because it has been proved in a study that if the people's heads were cooled by a cooling pack they yawned less – hot packs on the other hand, made them yawn more.

There appears to be some truth in the belief of yawning being contagious. Catriona Morrison at the University of Leeds has done research on this. She finds that contagious yawning indicates empathy. It indicates an appreciation of other people's behavioural and physiological state. There could well be an evolutionary reason for it. In early humans, yawn contagiousness might have helped people communicate their alertness levels to each other, and thus coordinate their sleep schedules. Or it could be part of a more general phenomenon of unconscious signals that serve to synchronise group behaviour, something that could have been essential for survival and works without understanding the action. A similar behaviour is seen with a flock of birds that rises to the air as soon as the first bird does so! There could be a simple biological reason too. In our brains we have something called mirror neurons. They are required because we learn many things by pure imitation. Language itself is learnt by imitation. Contagious yawning could be caused by mirror neurons. It is supported by the fact that autistic children do not show contagious yawning.

100

What Should You Do When Lightning Is Striking: Will You Be Safe Inside A Car?

A host of misconceptions abound regarding lightning strikes. If lightning is flashing, what you should do? Should you remain in the open or take a shelter. If you take a shelter, where should you go? Is it safe inside a car? Most people think that since a car is largely made of metal, it would be an easy target for lightning. It is not so. How?

Standing in the open is dangerous. Lightning can use you as a path to the earth just as easily it uses any other object. Never lie down on the ground. After lightning strikes the ground, there is an electric potential that radiates outwardly from the point of contact. If your body is in this area, current can flow through you. Trees are tall objects and have current conducting sap in them. Hence they attract lightning. Do not stand under a tree.

If you are inside a car, stay inside. Why? It is not because of the car standing on rubber tyres. In strong electric fields, rubber tyres actually become more conductive than insulating. You are safe in a car because the lightning will travel around the surface of the vehicle and then go to the ground. This occurs because the vehicle acts like a Faraday cage. Michael Faraday, a British physicist, discovered that a metal cage would shield objects within the cage when a high potential discharge hit the cage. The metal, being a good conductor, would direct the current around the objects and discharge it safely to the ground.

If you are indoors, stay off the landline phone. You can use a cordless phone or cell phone. If lightning strikes the phone line, the current will travel to every phone on the line (and potentially to you if you are holding the phone).

Stay away from plumbing pipes (bathtub, shower). Lightning has the ability to strike a house or near a house and impart an electrical charge to the metal pipes used for plumbing.

101

Can The Ray Guns Of Star Wars Be Made For Real?

If there is one thing that the world famous films of the Star Wars series and the immensely popular serial Star Trek have immortalised, it is undoubtedly the 'ray guns'. No one can forget the magic of the ray guns. The creators of the science fiction films imagined two types of weapons. The ray gun was more destructive. It could incinerate anything that it struck. The 'phaser' of the Star Trek serial was an anti-personnel weapon. It could either stun or kill a man depending on how it was configured.

The ray guns caught the fancy of billions. Even now many companies make toy ray guns. Readers may recall that under the Reagan administration, the US government spent trillions of dollars on research of what they called SDI (Strategic Defense Initiative). It was nothing but research on ray guns. The research is continuing even today. Now they call it research on 'directed energy weapons'.

The desire has always been the same. How do you shoot down a missile that is hurtling down on you with a hydrogen bomb? You could fire an anti-ballistic missile on it but chances are that it may be too late. After all there is a limit to its speed.

However, if you had a beam of energy travelling at the speed of light then things could be better. For the same reason, if you could have a pistol that fired a ray, it would be great.

Physicist William Broad has shown that there are practical problems in making ray guns. So lasers were the obvious choice. But the problem is that they consume a great deal of power and such power sources are too big. It is difficult to put them in satellites or even carry them on aircrafts. The laser is after all a form of light. This means that if the incoming missile has a mirror coating, your ray would be reflected off. It may even bounce back on you. Making lasers of X-rays and gamma rays that would penetrate metals is found very difficult.

102

Is There An X-Ray Or Some Other Imaging System That Can See Through Your Clothes?

Most people are familiar with regular X-rays used in radiological examinations. The technology of X-rays is quite simple. As we know, X-rays are electromagnetic waves of very high energy. In fact they have so high energy that they can penetrate through clothes as if clothes did not exist at all. The clothes are transparent to them. The X-rays penetrate most soft tissues also. However, the bones absorb them. In any case, different types of tissues absorb X-rays differently. The transmitted X-rays are recorded on a photographic film. That is how you are able to see your fractures in X-rays and diagnose other problems.

Could there be a system, which could reveal a naked body under the clothes. Surprisingly, yes! It is called 'backscatter imaging'. The secret of the backscatter imaging lies in the energy of the X-rays used. It uses X-rays of rather low energy. They are of so low energy that they cannot penetrate the muscle tissues at all. They would be totally absorbed in the body. Then how do they make use of them? The technique makes use of the X-rays, which are scattered or reflected after falling on the body. The reflection or scattering depends on the material from which the X-rays are reflecting. Thus they would be reflected differently from clothes and the body. If you filter out the reflections from the clothes, you get only the reflections from the body. They can be computer processed to produce a perfect image of the nude body under the clothes.

Backscatter imaging was developed to check terrorists who could have concealed explosives, etc. on their persons and which could have passed undetected under a usual metal detector. But it has raised serious privacy issue concerns. Critics in the USA have called it a virtual strip search that reduces the dignity of a person. The Americans are freely using it in Iraq but use in the USA is very limited.

103

Are You More Likely To Be Struck By Lightning If You Use A Mobile Phone During A Thunderstorm?

Many people believe that if one uses a mobile phone during a thunderstorm, he is more likely to be hit by lightning. This myth was propagated first in the USA. It caught on very quickly and soon the whole world started believing in it. A general advisory was issued in Australia. People even developed theories for the myth. It was said that usually when someone is struck by lightning, the high resistance of the skin conducts the flash over the body in what is known as a flashover. But if a metal object, such as a mobile phone, is in contact with the skin it disrupts the flashover and increases the odds of internal injuries and death.

When Ramsey M. Faragher of Cambridge investigated the matter he found that the myth was based on just three incidents that had taken place in Colorado and New Jersey. Now if only three incidents were registered in USA where hundreds of millions of people use mobile phones and lightning strikes nearly 30 million times per year, you can see for yourself that no inference can be drawn from it. Statistically, there is just not enough evidence.

Ramsey has further pointed out that the suggestion that the metal in a mobile phone is channelling the path of the current through the body is unlikely. The amount of metal in a typical mobile phone is very small compared to the amount of plastic in it; the key being the outer shell is usually all plastic. A typical mobile phone is better described as an insulator than a conductor.

Voltage in the cloud induces voltage in a metallic object. If the object is large and has sharp points then the intensity of the electric field becomes high enough for a discharge to take place. That is what happens with a lightning conductor. But holding a very small amount of metal inside an insulated plastic case is not likely to enhance the electric field enough to increase the risk of a strike much further.

104

Is It Possible To Travel To The Stars?

Who does not remember the world-famous science fiction TV series 'Star Trek' and the adventures of the American spaceship USS Enterprise as it travelled across the universe? *Space, the final frontier. These are the voyages of the starship Enterprise. Its five-year mission: To explore strange new worlds and to seek out new life and civilisations. To boldly go where no man has gone before.* Viewers were mesmerised.

Science fiction has led the common man to believe that it is indeed possible to travel to the distant stars and other galaxies provided we could build a rocket that travels fast enough. Many people keep on imagining that if we could build some antigravity device that could negate the effect of gravity, it would be possible for our rockets to break free of the gravitational pull of the earth. Whichever way you try, the Special theory of Relativity of Einstein dictates that no rocket can ever travel faster than the speed of light. That is the upper limit for anything that moves. The fastest rocket made so far, the Helios solar probe travelled at a speed of 70.2 km per second. The speed of light is 3 lakh km per second. Making that sort of progress is not possible.

There is another simple problem in the entire business of inter-galactic space travel. The problem is not that of speed, the problem is that of time. Outside our solar system, the nearest star Alpha Centauri is nearly 4.35 light years away from us. This means that even the light from Alpha Centauri takes more than four years to reach us. This means that even if we could build a rocket that travelled at only little less than the speed of light, it would take over four years to reach there. How would astronauts survive for such a long time? Then even radio communication will take eight years for one message to be answered. Other stars are thousands of light years away. There is no way one could go there or communicate with a rocket sent there.

105

Will An Aircraft Rupture And Fall Due To Pressurised Cabins If A Bullet Is Shot Through It From Inside?

This is one myth that has figured even in one of the James Bond movies. Most people believe that if a bullet is shot through the fuselage of an aircraft, the persons inside will be sucked out of the hole as the hole will keep on enlarging dramatically and may even cause the plane to eventually break apart. If you ask them as to how it would happen, they would say that the cabin of the aircraft is pressurised whereas the air outside at that height is very thin and hence there is a difference in pressures.

Well, there is a pressure difference all right but they miss out things. The first is that the pressure difference is not as large as they make it out to be. Secondly, the hole is quite small. Thirdly, and most importantly, the fuselage of an aircraft is neither a weak structure like the skin of a rubber balloon nor it is under tension. When you puncture a rubber balloon, the skin is already under tension because of having been stretched. This tension pulls the punctured skin apart with such force that it makes a tear much bigger than the hole you punctured.

Scientists took an old Hawaiian Airlines 737 in an airline graveyard in the Mohave Desert. They sealed it up and pumped the plane full of air using a massive air compressor until the difference between the interior of the plane and the air at sea level was the same, as it would be if the plane were flying at 35,000 feet. They put a crash-test dummy on a window seat and arranged for a bullet to be fired on the window. The air rushed out but even peanuts on the tray did not move, not to speak of the dummy. The dummy moved only when explosives blew up the entire window. Even then the hole did not enlarge and the dummy could not be sucked out.

There are proven instances where the plane was still able to maintain control and land even as it was shot up from inside.

106

Is There Any Good Reason For Mobile Phones To Be Not Used On Aircrafts?

Every time you sit in the aircraft, you are made to listen the annoying recording that you must switch off your mobile phones. The reason given is that they may interfere with navigational equipment of the aircraft.

This is a pure myth without any scientific basis and the companies have followed it blindly. Theoretically, any device that emits electromagnetic radiation can interfere with the functioning of other electronic devices. Spark plugs of motor vehicles create noise in radio receivers, so do the chokes of tube lights. Computers and remote control toys also generate electromagnetic radiation. But is there any reason to believe that the navigational equipments of the aircrafts are so unprotected that they would be affected by such tiny sources of electromagnetic radiation? Interference occurs only in those devices which are not electromagnetically shielded. Aircrafts are so important and costly that no electronic device in them can be left unprotected. Otherwise the best way to bring down an aircraft for a terrorist would have been to deposit a mobile phone in the luggage and leave it on. Then there would be no need of designing bombs and doing a 9/11 attack! But it does not happen. For God's sake, had it been possible, terrorists would have designed small radio transmitters that could be concealed in innocuous things like key rings, jewellery, cigarette case, cases of spectacles, etc. and crashed the planes.

A study in IEEE Spectrum has pointed that modern aircrafts and their electronic circuitry are designed to fly through thunderstorms which generate electromagnetic radiation which is billions of times stronger than the radiation of the mobile phones. Do you think the navigational equipment of an aircraft has ever malfunctioned simply because it flew through a thunderstorm?

In the history of aviation there has never been any accident which could be attributed to the use of mobile phone or any other electronic device on board. The simple fact is that the companies do not want to spend money on formal certification to prove that their equipments are electromagnetically shielded and adopt the short cut of banning mobiles.

107

Does A Bull Get Really Enraged On Seeing A Piece Of Red Cloth?

Ever since your childhood you must be hearing that if you show a piece of red cloth to a bull, the bull will be enraged. So much so that children who happened to wear red dresses were asked not to go in front of a bull or even a cow lest it irritates the animal. The myth has been used frequently in films also. Tamil films and films set in rural surroundings have been quite fond of this myth.

There is not even a grain of truth in it. Cows and bulls do not have colour vision. To them all the colors are same. Still, scientists disproved it. If waving a flag enrages a bull, it is the action of waving that irritates him because he takes that flag to be an enemy. It is quite like a cobra dancing to the pipe (been) of a snake charmer. The cobra cannot hear. However, the swaying motion of the snake charmer alerts him and he follows the movement so that it may not get attacked from an unexpected corner.

To test the myth of red cloth, scientists constructed three fake matadors that would carry different-coloured flags. First, they placed stationary flags of different colours near a bull. The bull charged the red, white and blue flags with equal ferocity even when all three flags were out at once. Using a remote controlled clothes line, the team proved that 'movement' rather than 'colour' angered the bulls. The scientists then placed the matador dummies in the ring, each one dressed in a different colour. The bull charged the white dummy first, the blue dummy second and the red dummy last. Finally, a scientist went into the ring dressed in a red jumpsuit and stayed still while two professional cowboys moved around the ring trying to draw the bull's attention. The bull chased the cowboys for a short time but ignored the scientist, which proved the theory that bulls concentrated on movement more than colour.

108

Is It Possible To Deceive A Breath Alcohol Analyser?

Drunken driving is one of the biggest problems in the world and causes most of the traffic accidents. Truck drivers are notorious for driving dead drunk. Drinking has fast become the way of life for the middle and upper classes. They feel superior to the poor truck drivers because they think that they are merely social drinkers and that they drink good quality liquor. The real fact is that even good quality alcohol has the same effect on human body, and social drinkers are as much at risk as anybody else. Merely because you are not slurring or swaying, it does not mean that alcohol has not had any effect on your reflexes.

The most effective tool in the hands of the police is the breath analyser. It works on the principle of electrochemical fuel cell technology. As the exhaled air from the suspect flows past one side of the fuel cell, the platinum oxidises any alcohol in the air to produce acetic acid, protons and electrons. The electrons flow through a wire from the platinum electrode. The wire is connected to an electrical current metre and to the platinum electrode on the other side. The more alcohol is oxidised, the greater the electrical current. A microprocessor measures the electrical current and calculates the alcohol in the breath.

It is the social drinkers who are bothered most about the breath analyser tests. They are afraid that if they get caught, it would be insulting for them. Hence to console themselves, they have developed several myths about the breath analysers. They believe that eating raw onions, using breath mints or mouthwash after drink can deceive the breath analyser. Such gimmicks can deceive the nose of the cop but not the machine.

Scientists have shown that if you use a mouthwash then you might register a higher reading on the machine because it contains alcohol and the vapour would go directly into the machine instead of coming through the blood in the lungs and the breath.

109

Will A Microwave Oven Explode If You Accidentally Place Some Metal In It?

The popular myth is that if by chance you happen to leave a metallic vessel or object in a microwave oven and run it, the microwave would explode. Do you think that a common household instrument could have been designed with such a great hazard?

What does a microwave oven consist of? The heart of a microwave oven is a microwave generator called magnetron. Microwaves are simple electromagnetic waves in a certain frequency range. What happens when electromagnetic waves from a radio station fall on the antenna of your radio receiver? The radio waves induce an oscillating voltage in it. That voltage is used to produce the sound. In a microwave oven, use is made of the fact that most food items have some water content. Here the water molecule plays an interesting role. It is a bipolar molecule. That is, it has a positive and a negative side. Hence they respond directly to the electric and magnetic components of the electromagnetic waves. When microwaves act on a food object, the water molecules start oscillating or vibrating with the frequency of the microwaves. Vibration of the water molecules results in internal friction, which produces heat and the food item is heated up. If the dish or any other thing has something in it, that could respond to the microwaves, that too would be heated up.

The oven has got very good reflectors so that the microwaves do not leak outside. What will happen if you keep a metallic object inside the oven and run it? Two things may happen. A voltage will be induced in the metallic object, which will obviously be higher than what is produced in normal food objects. Due to this, there may be sparking with the inner reflector wall. This sparking may ruin the reflector wall, that is all. Since some microwave energy may be reflected back into the magnetron, there may be some deleterious effect on the magnetron too. But there is no way the oven will explode.

110

Can Sharks Smell Human Blood From A Great Distance?

This is one of the most popular myths of the western world and has been accepted without question by all those who watch Hollywood films. A large number of films have been made on the terror of sharks, starting with the famous 'Jaws' series of films. The common theme in all such films is that the sharks can smell human blood from a great distance. If you have a slightest cut from a boat accident or any such thing, then the shark will smell you out from miles and appear from nowhere to gobble you up. According to such films, you are doomed if you happen to get injured in water; if you do not die of your injury, the shark will eat you up. The films generally make you believe that sharks can detect a single drop of blood in a pool of water and then they would be inexorably driven to eat you. But you never question the fact that human flesh is not the natural food of sharks – how could evolution give them the ability to sniff out human blood when it is only once in a blue moon that a shark gets to eat a human!

In fact such films have done a great disservice to the cause of animals, as they have made millions of people unnecessarily hostile to sharks. Hollywood has also done a similar disservice in respect of gorillas and anacondas through their Godzilla and anaconda films.

Scientists busted this myth by direct experiments. The sharks detected fish blood, however, they never detected human blood or did not care about it. Also, like any other scents, the sharks were not able to detect the blood until their noses came into contact with the blood particles, and the smell grew weaker as the blood got diluted by the water, meaning that a single drop of blood in a particular area of the pool would not be detectable by any shark that was not in that particular area nor swimming right into the blood.

111

Are The Fears Of Global Warming Justified?

Global warming is the biggest hoax of the 20th century. Not a shred of evidence has ever been produced to support it and yet it has been propagated so much that everyone accepts it as a fact. Sober scientists have concluded that much of the debate over global warming is predicated on fear, rather than science. To speak of global warming is fashionable and millions of dollars have been raised in its name. Global warming alarmists see a future plagued by catastrophic flooding, droughts, crop failures, mosquito-borne diseases and harsh weather – all caused by man-made greenhouse gas emissions. The simple fact is what we are witnessing is rather unusual climate changes in the world. Dr Michael Crichton, in his famous book *State of Fear*, has shown that there is no evidence to believe that even the unusual climate changes are due to man-made factors.

It is not global warming. In India, now we find harsher summers but very harsh winters too, and rain pattern has been disturbed also. Can you forget the increasing number of deaths due to cold wave that take place in North India every year; can you forget the increasing number of days engulfed by dense fog that lead to flight cancellations? South Africa has been getting terribly colder every year. The temperature of USA in April 2007 was the lowest in 113 years. To speak of global warming is utterly simplistic – it would mean that all that is happening is heating alone, though this is not so.

People frequently cite the example of the Arctic. The Climatologist George Taylor of Oregon State University has shown that Arctic temperatures are actually slightly cooler today than they were in the 1930s. Even hurricanes and tsunami were attributed to global warming. A team led by the National Oceanic and Atmospheric Administration's (NOAA) Dr Christopher Landsea concluded that there is no relation between global temperatures to hurricanes. Then people also speak of rise in sea level because of polar ice melting. In a study published this year in Global and Planetary Change, Dr Nils-Axel Morner of Sweden found that it is pure hoax.

112

Does CNG Really Cause Lesser Pollution Than Diesel?

All the buses in Delhi were made to change their fuel from diesel to CNG (compressed natural gas). The belief was that CNG pollutes less but there is no scientific basis of such a belief. Most people do not understand the mechanics of pollution. For them the smoke they see measures the degree of pollution. But there are many other pollutants too in the emission of engines. Visible smoke is the result of very small-suspended particles. CNG is better than diesel only in the sense that it produces less visible smoke than diesel; as far as other pollutants go, it produces even more! Unfortunately, people are not aware of them.

A new study shows that the combination of ultra-low-sulphur diesel (ULSD) with particulate matter (PM) trap actually produces less emission than CNG. The Swedish consultancy 'Ecotraffic' analysed actual exhaust gases of transit buses operating on diesel as well as alternative fuels including CNG, ethanol and biogas. Ecotraffic is one of Europe's most respected air pollution consultancies with previous studies for the Swedish EPA and the European Commission.

Their results were published by the Society of Automotive Engineers. It may be noted that Sweden has some of the world's toughest fuel and air pollution regulations, requiring ultra-clean Swedish Class 1 diesel. The study found that this ULSD, with less than 10 ppm sulphur, results in ultra-low emissions when combined with the Johnson-Matthey 'CRT' soot trap. One of the touted features of CNG is low emission of nitrogen oxides. The study has found that while CNG vehicles produce somewhat less nitrogen oxides on average, the great variability in their emissions raises serious questions about the long-term stability of the control systems.

CNG produces more of butadiene and polycyclic aromatic compounds (PACs). Pyrene, one of the PACs, is a dangerous cancer-producing substance. The study also notes that 'CNG has higher GHG (greenhouse gas) emissions than diesel fuel.' CNG also produces more aldehydes than trap-equipped diesel engines. The study concludes that the lowest cancer risk index is clean-diesel with PM trap, compared to CNG, ethanol or biogas.

113

Can Our Energy Problems Be Solved By Solar Power?

These days it is fashionable to tout solar energy as the panacea for all energy-related problems. It is projected as a clean source of energy whereas thermal power is treated as a pollutant of atmosphere. Most people do not know that while the total amount of solar energy reaching the planet is very high, it comes so diffused that when collected at a place which is practicably as large as it could be, the energy is very little.

There are two methods of generating electricity from sunlight, one which employs photovoltaic cells to convert light into direct-current electricity. On the micro-scale, photovoltaic cells power our calculators, which require only a few thousandths of a watt to operate. Orbiting spacecraft and remote monitoring stations have successfully used this technology for years with peaks of several hundred watts. The trouble occurs when very large amount of power needs to be generated and made available at all times.

The energy of the sun shining down on a unit area of the Earth varies according to the location on Earth, the time of day, the season and weather conditions. In order to calculate the average output from a photovoltaic array, one would take the falling energy per square metre or acre, allow for needed spacing, and multiply by the efficiency of the photovoltaic cell. Let us check what power could be generated in a desert. Commercial photovoltaic cells turn about 10 per cent of the sun's energy into electrical energy, and in order to keep the PV cells clean and to direct them toward the sun, 50 per cent spacing is typical. An acre of land with solar-cell arrays of 50 per cent spacing would theoretically produce an average of 48.5 kW. That is enough for about 40 hand-held hair dryers only but to get it requires an area which is four-fifth the size of a football field covered with expensive semiconductors and miles of inter-wiring, not to mention inverters and transformers to produce usable electricity. It will be worse in other areas.

Solar energy is good for small electronic devices and satellites, whereas it is not practical for domestic and commercial use.

Part VII

ASTROLOGY

114

Can Tarot Cards Tell Your Future And Help You Solve Your Problems?

The basic idea behind the tarot is very simple – a deck of tarot cards is made up of 78 cards, each of which has a specific meaning relating to a particular concept of life, or experience. In a tarot reading, the cards are shuffled and then laid out in a 'spread' – a pattern on a table, where each position represents a particular aspect of life, for instance 'the recent past' or 'current emotions'. The reader then looks at how the meaning of a card corresponds to the position it is in, and tells the client what the spread appears to be saying about their current state of life.

The whole thing is utter nonsense. The cards do not have a mind of their own nor are they imbued with any divine powers. How can they arrange themselves into a pattern, which will tell about your present or future? How can the cards arrange themselves into a 'meaningful pattern'? Why should some pieces of cardboard with pretty pictures on them be able to mysteriously rearrange themselves into an order to tell us about our life and experiences? The tarot card readers are not able to explain how the cards can arrange themselves – they attribute it to some mysterious force, which even they do not know.

The fact is that the cards will, at best, be arranged randomly. It will then be left to the card reader to interpret them in any way he wants. That way tarot reading is just a fancy and costlier version of the country astrologer and his parrot found in fairs of small towns. Does not the astrologer leave you partly satisfied? They speak in vague terms and some things do fit in your life. They would say that there is some person in your life who is jealous of you and wants to harm you. Don't we all have such persons in our lives? And you tend to believe in them. When they say that your good time will start shortly – does that not make you happy?

115

Can Feng Shui Be Of Any Help In Your Life?

The literal meaning of the words feng shui is 'wind-water'. Believers of feng shui say that it is an ancient Chinese practice of placement and arrangement of space to achieve harmony with the environment. Proponents claim that feng shui has an effect on health, wealth and personal relationships. The goal of feng shui is to situate the living/working place and the surroundings made by humans on spots with good qi (a mysterious energy).

Like many farcical things, feng shui has also resulted in good business for unscrupulous companies. So, now they sell feng shui objects which, if placed in your bedroom, drawing room or wherever, would improve your life. While the ancient Chinese believed that good feng shui would produce bountiful harvest, healthy livestock and abundant life, these days you have feng shui objects which claim to improve even your love life, relationships and so on.

As any sensible man can see, there is no way the mere placement of a flower vase, crystal, wind chime, mirrored balls, mirrors or some decorative object in a particular place could change your nature, disposition, or fortunes. It is even more improbable that their supposedly wrong placement could adversely affect your fortunes. Even in its own land, the Chinese government officially describes it as a 'feudalistic superstitious practice'.

Feng shui caters to the inherent insecurity in the mind of a man. All of us have problems in our lives. However, most of us are not prepared to accept that as many of them could be due to some inadequacy in our own selves. We are only too willing to accept that the problems could be due to something else which is not connected with us. That saves our egos from getting hurt and in fact gives us a great solace that the nagging problem was really due to the bed facing in the wrong direction. Feng shui, therefore, does harm to us as it does not let us concentrate on our shortcomings.

116

Can Crystal Ball Gazers Tell Your Future?

This is one of the oldest frauds in the western world. Many fashionable women have started doing it in India and the astrology section of lifestyle magazines have usually a crystal ball reader also. More than two thousand years before Christ, the Celtic priests called Druids used to do it. Later it became synonymous with the gypsies, witches and magicians. Of late it has caught the fancy of the people again, courtesy the Harry Potter books and films.

Crystal balls are made of beryl, quartz, rock crystal or even transparent rock. The crystal ball gazer puts it on a stand or table or just holds it in his hands. They keep a blue or black velvet cloth under it. The reading is done in a quiet dark room with a couple of candles, which add to the mystic atmosphere. The crystal gazers claim that they go into a trance and then see your past, present or future in the crystal.

Nothing could be more ridiculous. Even high school students of science know how images are produced. There is no way that miniaturised images of someone's past, present and future would appear inside a crystal ball. No crystal gazer has ever been able to demonstrate those images or produce a photographic or video record of the images. This means that he alone is able to see them. If the crystal gazer claims to see something which no one else can see, it can mean only one thing – he is hallucinating or telling a white lie.

Crystal gazing is a lot more ridiculous than simple astrology. Astrologers believe that planets affect human lives and their position determines what sort of effect they would have. They only tell the effects; they do not claim to actually 'see' the effects. They would only say that you are likely to get married but the crystal gazer claims to actually see you in a bridal dress!

Part VIII

MEDICINE

117

If A Pregnant Woman Eats Papaya, Will It Lead To Miscarriage?

It has been believed for long in the Indian subcontinent and even in Africa that if a pregnant woman eats papaya, it will lead to miscarriage. The argument given is that papaya generates heat or that it is a hot food. This myth has figured in films as well as TV serials. The fact is that 100 grams of papaya give only 27 calories. Thus it is not a hot food. Incidentally, it is because of the low calorie value that papaya is recommended for diabetics. Ghee, oil, dry fruits and sugar have much higher calorie values but are not abortifacient.

Then, is there any such chemical in papaya that could cause miscarriage? A research was done in the University of Lagos to clarify this point. They found that there is nothing in the papaya that could cause miscarriage. Then they shifted their research to the seeds of papaya. They took out the extract of papaya seeds and administered them to pregnant rats in doses ranging from 100 mg/kg body weight. It was found that in low doses, it had no effect at all. But in high doses it adversely affected the growth of the fetuses and in some cases they aborted too. The first point to be noted is that in the experiment they had used the extract of papaya seeds to feed the rats because you cannot force the rats to eat seeds directly. It takes a lot of seeds to get the extract. Humans are not likely to eat so many seeds that they would get the equivalent of nearly 50 grams of extract. In fact the total amount of seeds in one fruit does not come to 50 grams, not to speak of their extract. Unless one is a complete fool, no human ever eats the seeds of papaya. Even if someone eats a few seeds by mistake, she is not likely to get even a few milligrams of the extract of the seeds.

118

Can Hair Oil Reduce Mental Tension?

The advertisement of a certain brand of hair oil shows a popular actor posing as a PA or peon and advising his boss to use the hair oil because it reduces mental tension. The punch line of the advertisement is: *Tension ko pension dijiye.* Earlier it used to be another actor singing: *Thanda thanda cool cool.* If you pay attention you will see that the hair oil has increased its audacity over the years. Earlier they sold it only as hair oil that gave a cooling sensation. Now they are selling it as a medicine, something which can reduce tension and stress! There are other oils also which make similar claims.

The company claims that nine ayurvedic herbs have been used in the hair oil and it helps in getting rid of headache and sleeplessness. The company has not produced any study of controlled clinical trials in respect of its claims. Scientific analysis has shown that the cooling sensation of the hair oil comes from the mint oil in it, quite like peppermint in mouth. It has no other function or therapeutic value.

Mental tension and stress are highly subjective affairs. Generally, a tensed or stressed out man can feel better merely by lying down for a while or talking to someone sympathetic. A little bit of pampering may also help. In fact that is why mothers press the heads of their tensed children. A hair oil massage does no more. There is no evidence that hair oil penetrates the skin or that its herbs can reach the blood circulation. Headaches are caused by numerous serious ailments also. You could have a headache due to something as simple as sinusitis to as serious as a growing tumour. Both require internal medication. No amount of hair oil with herbs in it can help. But serious mental tension does not go unless the root problem is solved. Suppose someone's mother is sick and he has no money to spend on her treatment, resulting in great tension; will his tension be eased by applying the hair oil while his mother lies sick? Certainly not!

119

Is A Chyawanprash Containing Gold And Silver Any Better Than Ordinary Chyawanprash?

Chyawanprash as a general health tonic has got a huge market due to aggressive marketing by the companies. Chyawanprash's claim to fame rests on its having been discussed in the Charak Samhita. But the fact is that the original recipe of the Charak Samhita contains a long list of herbs, many of which do not even exist now. The Medicinal Natural Products Research Laboratory, Mumbai and the Potdar Ayurvedic Medical College, Mumbai have done research on the commercial preparations of Chyawanprash and they found that there is no way one can make Chyawanprash by following the original formula simply because all the herbs are just not available. Therefore, strictly speaking, what is sold by the name of Chyawanprash is not really Chyawanprash. Companies, which sell Chyawanprash now, make them by a simplified formula which is their own invention in which taste takes precedence over therapeutic value and even preservatives like potassium sorbate are added. They are thus a far cry from the original prescription of Charak. There is no standardisation either, as each company follows its own recipe; if every product were to be made according to the book, they could not differ so much in taste and cost!

Some companies claim to have added metals like gold and silver to their Chyawanprash. Charak has not prescribed using metals in Chyawanprash anywhere. Hence their claim that '*Sona de surakshit tan, chandi de tez dimaag*' does not have the authority of Charak in support. They do not even tell in which form gold and silver have been used in it, or how much of them is used and how do they fix the cost? Ayurveda recommends the use of metal 'bhasmas' but only for specific purposes and not for vague claims like 'surakshit tan', i.e. a healthy body – for that matter the entire Ayurveda deals with healthy body only. When Charak never claimed that silver could increase your mental powers, how could a company do so?

On the other hand, there has never been any scientific study regarding the value of metals in Ayurveda. Rather, there are many instances of heavy metal poisoning.

120

Are Cough Drops And Cough Mixtures Of Any Real Therapeutic Value?

Cough drops have a huge market. They indulge in very aggressive advertising of the type: 'vicks ki goli lo khich khich dur karo'. The consumer is made to believe that these are instant cure to sore throat and cough. This is purely a marketing gimmick. Scientists have refuted the claims strongly.

Most so-called medicated cough drops are usually small, sweetened (often with artificial sweeteners) candies, and contain substances like menthol. Menthol, as we all know, produces a soothing sensation because it is a mild anaesthetic. But that does not cure the underlying cause of the sore throat or cough. In fact the same relief can be obtained by sucking on any piece of hard candy. Whether you suck on a medicated cough drop or ordinary candy, they both work by stimulating the flow of saliva which keeps the throat moist. There is no other function. There is nothing in any cough drop which can attack the root cause of sore throat or cough. Licking honey will coat the throat and keep it moist for a little while. Then it will be swallowed automatically. The same effect is obtained by drinking any hot drink, soup, or syrupy substances.

Most of the over-the-counter cough mixtures are equally useless. Researchers of the University of Bristol have shown in a study published in the British Medical Journal that most cough medicines are no better than placebos. The American College of Chest Physicians have pointed out that many cough mixtures are in fact an illogical combination. They contain both expectorant and suppressant. The expectorant loosens the mucus so that it may be expelled by the action of coughing. A cough suppressant suppresses the desire to cough. Thus they work against each other. One should take either an expectorant or a suppressant depending on whether he has productive or dry cough. The journal 'Chest' concludes that there is no scientific evidence that cough suppressants, such as dextromethorphan, or expectorants, such as guaifenesin, relieve coughs that are the result of colds.

121

Does Laughter Therapy Have Any Use?

This is one of the latest fads and has hit major cities and small towns alike. At such places you find laughter clubs where children, young and old, men and women assemble in the morning and laugh like crazy. Even yoga gurus have started laughter therapy and they call it 'haasya asana'.

We are very much aware of the old adage: laughter is the best medicine. Unfortunately, it is only an adage. Laughter can be of help only when it comes from within, such as when you read a very funny joke or watch a good comedy or when you are genuinely happy for whatever reason. That type of laughter is spontaneous and comes from within. Such laughter comes because the joke or the comedy has really made you happy. It makes you feel good; it may even make you forget your sorrows and tension for some time. Thus it can be argued that genuine laughter has a good effect on you. It has been found to reduce neuroendocrine and stress-related hormones.

But nothing is to be gained by artificial laughter. Even if you make ha-ha-ha sounds, or you open your mouth wide, or if you clutch your abdomen, you cannot fool your inner self; you cannot make yourself happy by making laughing sounds. You would be doing merely a mechanical act. Suppose your child is lying seriously sick at home and you are deeply worried. Can you make yourself happy by going to the park and making ha-ha sounds with your neighbours? Will the worry of your child leave you even for a moment? Genuine happiness must come first – genuine laughter follows that. There cannot be a genuine laughter without genuine happiness. Still, even genuine laughter cannot produce happiness. So there is no question of genuine happiness coming from artificial laughter.

Such fraud is being perpetrated in the name of laughter therapy that they have started claiming that it improves your immunity and intellectual performance also.

122

Is Taking Antibiotics In Viral Fevers Of Any Help At All?

These days who does not suffer from viral fevers? Viral fevers of all types have become so widespread that one gets them at least once a year. They are so distressing due to pain in the joints, sore throat and weakness that patients become restless. Indian doctors have fallen into the habit of prescribing antibiotics freely for viral fevers. This is against scientific opinion.

Bacteria are tiny single-celled organisms. They can exist independently but they thrive only inside the body of a host. When they invade a body, they multiply. In a healthy body, unless the infection is very severe, they are dealt by the body's own immune mechanism which produces antibodies. If that were not adequate then we take antibiotics, which either kill the bacteria outright or inhibit their multiplication.

Viruses, on the other hand, are just small packets of protein with genetic material. Viruses can exist independently but they cannot reproduce. To reproduce they must invade a cell. Thus there is a basic difference in the reproduction of bacteria and viruses. Bacteria are self-sufficient creatures, which multiply outside our cells; viruses multiply inside our cells.

Antibiotics are of no use against viruses because they never reach the viruses, which are hidden inside your cells. Now you can understand why it is difficult to kill viruses – you would kill your own cells in the process. The body kills them itself using its T-lymphocytes. And that is why most viral infections are self-limiting. There are special and costly antiviral drugs, which act by interfering with viral enzymes; they are available only for few viruses.

Scientists maintain that treatment of viral fever is purely symptomatic with antipyretic and analgesic drugs. Bed rest and adequate fluid intake is advised. Nasal decongestants may be beneficial. Specific antiviral therapy is not routinely recommended. Only in cases of super-infection do antibiotics need to be prescribed. Also please keep in mind that by taking antibiotics in advance you cannot prevent super-infection.

123

Can You Catch A Cold By Going Out In Cold Weather?

Since generations, mothers have told their kids not to go out in cold without a sweater otherwise they will 'catch cold'. This is a great misconception. 'Common cold' or flu is an infection whereas exposure to cold is quite another thing. One does not get 'common cold' or flu merely by going out in cold weather.

The fact is that the only way to catch a cold or flu is by picking up a virus. Viruses are more easily shared when people are clustered together indoors. You do not have to wait to be sneezed on to catch a cold or flu – you can pick the virus up right from a counter top, keyboard, telephone or other surface. Rhinoviruses, the family of germs responsible for most colds, have been shown to survive on a surface for several hours or even days. Dr Richard Rosenfeld, professor and chairman of otolaryngology at Long Island College Hospital in Brooklyn, N.Y. says: "Even if there is just a little left and you happen to touch that doorknob or coffee cup, the virus can then survive on your hands for quite a long time. Then all it takes is a little wipe of your nose or eyes, and whatever little bit of virus is there, it will go to town very quickly.. It is a very efficient multiplying process."

If the human body is exposed for considerable time to extreme cold weather, the following things may happen. Frostnip is the freezing of the top layer of skin tissue and is normally reversible. It mostly affects the cheeks, earlobes, fingers and toes. Frostbite is the actual freezing of the tissue and/or body part. Ice crystals form inside the skin that can destroy the tissues, and you could lose skin. It affects the ears, nose, fingers and toes most often. Hypothermia is the general cooling of the body. When the body temperature drops much below the normal temperature of 98.6° Fahrenheit, serious problems can arise. Severe hypothermia can lead to death. But still you would not 'catch cold'.

124

Can You Get Leucoderma If You Eat Fish And Milk Together?

One of the highly prevalent myths is that you will get leucoderma if you eat fish and milk together. Leucoderma is also known as vitiligo. In this, one develops white patches on the skin. Even now many people confuse it with leprosy though it has no connection. Leucoderma is an internal disorder and not a disease like leprosy which is caused by an external organism.

How does our skin get its colour? It gets it because of a pigment called melanin. Melanin is produced in the skin by the cells called melanocytes. What happens in leucoderma is that the production of the skin-colouring pigment, melanin is reduced. This shows up prominently as white patches in dark-skinned people but even white-skinned people develop this condition. The exact cause still remains unknown. However, there are theories suggesting autoimmune link, hormonal connection, etc. There is no evidence that any particular food item can trigger it.

Scientists have investigated the myth of fish and milk being eaten together. In India and Pakistan the myth is so strong that hardly anybody would dare to eat them together. But elsewhere in the world, it is quite common. In neighbouring Bangladesh they are commonly eaten together. In the western world there are a large number of recipes where milk and fish are used together. They include fish sticks with milk; fish and clam chowders in milk-based stock for roux; baked milkfish; fish pie; and fish poached in milk, etc. Yet from no corner of the world, it has been reported that they suffer from a higher incidence of leucoderma because of this.

Certain food items may not go well with some people; they may get an upset stomach or even gastritis. Some people may be allergic to certain foods and may develop severe allergy from them. But that does not mean that such food items are uniformly bad for the entire human race! And, there is no reason to believe that such foods may cause melanocytes to stop producing melanin.

125

Does Massage Have Any Therapeutic Value At All?

Everyone is aware of massage. Massage is indeed pleasurable. That is why rich men used to keep servants for massaging them. Wrestlers used to get massaged by their students. These days there are many massage parlours. It feels good to be taken care of by someone. If you are tired, it feels even better. There are physiotherapists to massage sportspersons.

We do not have any problems with massage as a pleasurable or relaxing activity. It also reduces local pain. However, the claims of any therapeutic value to massage are absolutely unscientific. Massage therapists claim that massage is like tuning a car and that it helps in medical conditions like allergies, asthma, bronchitis, spastic colon, constipation, diarrhoea and sinusitis. This is not possible. Any external manipulation of the soft tissues of the body or application of pressure on muscles or manipulation of joints cannot have any effect on any internal problem including allergies or infections. If massage therapists claim that it works, then they must demonstrate it in clinical trials and double-blind experiments. The American Massage Therapy Association has never taken up this challenge.

In India, ayurvedic massage is big business for hotels and resorts. There are many tourists who return satisfied. The reason is that they never had any problem. The tourists who come to such resorts are stressed-out people. What actually work for them are the forced rest of two weeks or so and not the massage. Many of them are highly susceptible people. Then there is the very aggressive marketing of ayurvedic massage which makes them believe that the ancient Indian science would actually work. Most of them do not even know whether they are being given ayurvedic abhyanga massage or Swedish massage or Chinese massage or just some pampering in fancy setting with fancy oils and fragrances. Hence actually there is a placebo effect.

Massage can in fact be very harmful if someone is suffering from deep vein thrombosis, bleeding disorders (or taking blood thinners such as Warfarin), damaged blood vessels, weakened bones from cancer, osteoporosis, or fractures, and fever.

126

Are Angioplasty And Stents As Useful As They Are Claimed To Be?

The doctors nowadays make you believe that angioplasty and stents are synonymous with treatment for heart diseases. Angioplasty is the mechanical widening of a narrowed or totally-obstructed blood vessel. A stent is a small, lattice-shaped, metal tube that is inserted permanently into an artery. The stent helps to open an artery so that the blood can flow through it. Scientists of the Harvard Medical School have found that angioplasty and stents help only in the case of sudden blockage of a coronary artery, and many of the angioplasties and stents are unnecessary and are done because they generate good business for cardiac surgeons and hospitals.

How are patients hooked up for angioplasties and stents? Suppose someone goes for a treadmill test or has some chest pain and if his results are not perfectly normal then an angiogram is taken and a stent is inserted next. Does it help? No! Dr Thomas Lee of the Brigham Hospital says that a big narrowing on a coronary angiogram only tells that a patient has atherosclerosis. For every big atherosclerotic plaque, there are dozens of smaller ones. These small atherosclerotic plaques are as likely as big ones to rupture and cause a blood clot that kicks off a heart attack.

And because small plaques are more common than big ones, most heart attacks actually begin with rupture of a small plaque. Hence quashing that big plaque against the wall with a stent does not make the other plaques go away, or reduce the risk of heart attack. After all how many stents can they place?

The correct medical advice for people who have abnormal exercise tests and coronary angiograms is that they must reduce their risk of a heart attack by controlling their blood pressure, cholesterol and other risk factors. In short, they must be helped while going after the widespread problem of atherosclerosis, and not by focusing on the biggest atherosclerotic plaque. Researchers have found that in people with stable angina, taking oral medication is just as good as having an angioplasty and a stent.

127

Is It Hygienic To Pick Up And Eat A Dropped Food Item Within Five Seconds?

Suppose you have a food item in your hand or plate. Suddenly it falls down, what do you do? Of course, if it were a liquid item, most sensible people would forget about it. Similarly, if the item has fallen on a road, people would forget it. The trouble arises when the food item is dry or has fallen in your home on the floor, which you supposedly keep clean. What do you do with that? This confusion prevails all over the world. In fact, folklore has invented even a rule, which they call 'five-second rule'. The idea is that if you pick up the item within five seconds, it is good enough to eat it.

There is no scientific basis of such a myth. The fact is that in spite of what they show in the advertisements for floor cleaners, the floor is never free of bacteria like E. Coli. The bacteria come in force as soon as you step on the floor wearing shoes, which is a storehouse of bacteria. Even if you keep your shoes outside the house and you come in wearing socks, the sweat-soaked socks harbour bacteria. Unless you wash your feet before entering the house, you carry bacteria with you. Secondly, it has been shown that bacteria cling to a food item very quickly. Dr Philip Tierno of New York University conducted experiments and found that the number of bacteria found after a fraction of a second was nearly the same as that found after five seconds. Scientists also found that bacteria are extremely small and are not removed by blowing on a dry food item or wiping it.

Dry foods, of course, get fewer bacteria and unless your immunity is weakened, you may not fall sick by eating a biscuit that had fallen. But the five-second rule has no basis.

128

Do Popular Hangover Remedies Really Work?

What is hangover? Those who drink alcohol to excess know it well. The most common symptoms are: headache, nausea and grogginess. Most scientists believe that they are caused by a combination of factors resulting from intoxication by alcohol, including dehydration, dilation of blood vessels around the brain, changes in certain chemical levels in the body and alteration of the sleep cycle. Down the ages, a host of conventional and folk remedies have been tried for hangover. However, scientific research has proved that none of them actually work. The surest way to avoid hangover is to drink in moderation.

Popular hangover remedies range from simple things in the kitchen like coffee, waffle sandwiches, fried egg sandwiches, vanilla milkshake, a glass of beer mixed with 7-Up to herbal or vegetable products like artichoke extract, sarsaparilla root, and prickly pear to exotic things like the hair of dog, pickled sheep eyeballs in tomato juice and a brew of the dung of rabbit. Many people have taken medicines like paracetamol, multivitamins or even saline drips.

None of them have stood the test of scientific scrutiny. Those who claim that some particular concoctions have worked for them either tell lies or make themselves believe that they work, blind faith being their most potent ingredient.

A very detailed study by British and Dutch researchers revealed some but not compelling evidence in support of a yeast product called borage and a painkiller medicine called tolfenamic acid.

They advise that women should not drink more than three units per day and the upper limit for men is four. Now one unit is not one peg, chhota or Patiala. One unit is an amount of drink that contains 8 grams of pure alcohol. Most whiskeys and rum in India have 43% alcohol v/v. This means that 8 grams of alcohol would come to 23.8 ml. Thus four units make for 95.2 ml. This will be about one and a half large peg of 60 ml. Exceed that and you are risking your health.

129

Is Aromatherapy Of Any Use At All?

Look up any fashion or lifestyle magazine and you will find many references to aromatherapy. Costly spas offer it. One can even purchase the oils and do it himself. The claim that it promotes health and well-being, relaxes the body and mind, enhances mood, purifies the air, acts as antidotes to air pollution, relieves fatigue, tones the body, nourishes the skin, promotes circulation, alleviates feminine cramps, and do about 50 other things. They also claim that inhaling the scents 'balances the biological background,' 'revitalises the cells,' and produces a 'strong energizing effect on the sympathetic nervous system.' The claims are based on the assumption that oils contain the life force, spirit, or soul of the plant.

As you can see, all such things are highly subjective. Giving even simple rest to a stressed-out man can make him feel good. If he has taken a break from his routine he will feel even better. Anybody who is given a break from the daily cooking, washing, household chores, office and travel will feel better. And for that they give credit to aromatherapy because they charge heavily for it! A clever way of making fools of rich people!

What is aromatherapy? It has been described as making money out of scents. They use oils derived from plants (say, for example, sandalwood oil) and use them for inhalation, massage, or other applications to the skin. They call them 'essential oils'. This is misleading. The word 'essential' does not refer to nutritional value but to the volatile, aromatic components that are the 'essence' of the plant. Pleasant odours can be enjoyable and may enhance people's efforts to relax. However, there is no evidence or reason that aromatherapy products provide the health benefits claimed by their proponents. How can a scent cur a medical condition?

In fact Morse Mehrban challenged the claims of an American company Aroma Vera, Inc., of Los Angeles in the court and the company had to pay damages for false claims.

130

Is Watching TV Safe For Kids Below Three Years Of Age?

No, no, we are not talking of adult films, music videos, violence or the Fashion TV. We are talking of the effect of the regular TV on your kid. Many parents have the habit of plopping their kids in front of the TV to stop them from crying. Researchers have found that the more television the children watch, the more likely they are to later become fidgety, impulsive and have difficulty concentrating – all core symptoms of ADHD (attention-deficit/hyperactivity disorder, sometimes abbreviated ADD). A study published in the April 2004 issue of Pediatrics concluded that exposure to television in children aged 1- to 3-year-old increased the risk of developing attention-related problems at age 7. In follow-up studies, the researchers found that early TV viewing was also associated with cognitive trouble and problems in school as children matured.

Dr Dimitri Christakis of the University of Washington explains that a zoned-out, transfixed gaze that comes over your kid's face is the precise effect intended by many TV producers. When fast edits and scene changes flash across the screen, the brain works hard to comprehend them. As the cuts are so unlike real life or real time, the viewer is focused but not actually concentrating or comprehending. This phenomenon, known as the orienting reflex, may contribute to a child's impatience with the slow and impossibly dull real world.

Television has often been cited as a source of information or an aid to brain development. It is not really so. Dr Christakis says that good television is best used in tandem with good parenting. There are things a parent can do early in life to promote the development of attention. Certain activities like reading to a child or taking a child to the zoo are associated with increased attention later in life. In the early age, a kid should be provided with informational input only at a rate that is commensurate with his capacity – the TV unleashes a virtual bombardment and that leads to problems.

Part IX

SPORTS AND MARTIAL ARTS

131

Is There Anything Mysterious About The Breaking Of Tiles, Boards And Slabs By Karate Practitioners?

One of the most impressive shows of karate and other martial arts consists of breaking wooden boards, ice, slabs, etc. Most people get the impression that karate masters have some mysterious powers. They also support the myth by claiming that they are using the energy called *ki* or *chi*.

There is nothing mysterious about breaking things. Physicists Jearl Walker of Cleveland State University and John Chananie of University of Virginia have done research on this. They have shown that some very clever tricks are used in breaking. No karate master has ever demonstrated breaking standardised materials. They always bring their own material. When they are breaking wooden boards they ensure that they use a light wood like pinewood and not heavy wood like teak. One who breaks a stack of pinewood easily would break his hand if he tries to break a stack of teakwood. Even for pinewood, they very cleverly hit along the grain. Spectators are not able to notice this. You see, light wood like pine is very weak along the grains but strong across the grains. The wood is fibrous and the fibres do not bind strongly with each other along their lengths. But when you try to break them across, then this weak binding does not matter. When they are breaking tiles, the tiles are either soaked in water or engine oil or simply overbaked to the point of becoming brittle. For any stack they leave spacers between boards or tiles. The effect is that each slab is hit not only by the hand but also by the hard edges of the board or tile above it. Give them a solid stack and their hands would break. When they use ice, they use porous ice or an ice block which had been hammered in the centre and then re-frozen. When they use bricks, they use poor quality bricks.

This does not mean that karate masters are not strong. It requires mental conditioning to hit something and overcome the pain and fear of getting hurt. But it is true that they do not have any superhuman strength.

132

Do Martial Artists Possess Any Mysterious Energy Called 'Chi'?

Martial artists like to maintain an air of mystery around their activities. It is true that they train very hard and some of them are very strong also. But their habit is that they attribute their feats to a mysterious energy called chi or ki. The claim is that by harnessing this energy their punches get power.

Interestingly such claims are made only by old masters of Chinese, Japanese or Korean origin. Such men are a little reclusive by their nature. They wish to add to their mystique by such claims. Some of them have gone to the extent of claiming that by using their chi energy they can hasten recovery; one burn victim even claimed to have healed himself in a matter of a few days whereas normally it would have taken a couple of months. Some of them claim that they can make themselves so heavy that they cannot be moved.

Men like Bolo Yeung, Van Damme and Chick Norris who are champion martial artists have never made any such claim. The simple fact is that they are indeed very strong men. Bob Sapp is a mixed martial arts practitioner and his technique is so poor that it appears like a schoolboy fighting, yet he hits them so hard that it is difficult to stand up to him.

Old masters never tell: Where is that? What is that? What does it do? Science does not admit of any energy called *chi*, hence there is no secret energy flowing in the human body which will flow through your hands into the opponent's face. The Chinese have known *chi* for long now and had it been really useful in accelerated healing they would have been using it instead of modern medicine. Honest martial artists also have rejected the *chi* theory; they depend on their muscle power. They have also shown that many of the feats of old masters are performed on willing and cooperative disciples. They throw themselves with the slightest motion of the master.

133

Is There Any Significance Of The Loud Shout Of The Martial Artists When They Punch Or Kick?

Martial artists shout loudly when they punch or kick. The shout is known as kiai in the parlance of martial arts. What is its use? They try to give a mystical explanation to it. It is claimed that the shout or kiai facilitates the flow of the mysterious energy called 'chi' and that is what gives power to their strikes.

The simple fact is that the kiai only serves the function of distracting or startling the opponent. If you remember any of the Bruce Lee films, you would recall that he used to make strange sounds. When Bruce Lee used to make those meowing like sounds, he did that only as a style statement and for theatrical effect. He never claimed that his punches got power from them.

Kiai supporters say that the sound or kiai is to be released with the exhalation of breath which contracts internal muscle around areas of the diaphragm and projects the energy (chi) from that source. The amount of energy or chi projected depends on how shallow, deep, hard or soft the exhalation is. This did not stand up to the test of science. In the first place there is no evidence of anything called the 'chi'. Exhalation is fine and the abdominal muscles also contract when one shouts, but that may help him in only one way. If he were struck in the abdomen at that time, he would be hurt less. But experiments showed that there was no effect on the power of the punch, whether one shouted or not. Shouting is just for dramatic effect. It may convey the impression that one is using great power. It is for this reason that many tennis players these days, both men and women, have started grunting loudly. They are no better than those who play quietly. Boxers keep their mouth shut – would any karate practitioner take a quiet punch from a heavyweight champion boxer and remain standing? Incidentally judo masters do not shout at all though they too claim to use chi.

134

The Famous Skull Mark Made By The Punch Of Phantom – Can It Be Ever Made In Real Life?

One of the most popular comic book heroes across the world is the Phantom created by Lee Falk. The Phantom wears a tight-fitting purple dress and a mask, and is constantly protecting the world from the criminals. Phantom is popular because he is closer to real life. Unlike the Superman, he does not come from the planet Krypton and does not fly in air. Unlike Mandrake the Magician, he does not depend on magic. There is, however, one thing unnatural about the Phantom. The most famous feat of Phantom is that he knocks out the opponents with one clear punch to the jaw. He does not indulge in any prolonged fight with his opponents – all he needs is one punch. The punch is so hard that the skull mark engraved on his ring is permanently made on the jaw of the criminal. The Phantom says that it takes years for that mark to go and till such time, the man carries a living advertisement that he was a criminal whom Phantom had punished. The question is: Is it really possible to hit somebody so hard that the ring on his finger would leave an indelible mark on his skin as if it were a tattoo?

Scientists tested it by direct experiment. A human skull was taken with a pigskin stretched on it to resemble human skin. A ring was made of sterling silver with a skull mark engraved on it quite like the Phantom's. Scientists knew that if they were to hit the dummy themselves, it could be alleged that they could not hit it hard enough. Hence they made a robot which could punch harder than even professional boxers. Still the ring did not leave any mark. However, when it did leave a mark, it was found that the skull was also crushed. Thus the inference is that the Phantom's ring cannot leave a mark. If Phantom indeed punches very hard, the criminals would get killed due to the fractured skull and would not be alive to show the mark to the world.

135

Are The Violent Throws And Strikes Made In Pro-Wrestling Real?

Who has not seen pro-wrestling and its violent throw and strikes? Remember those wrestlers who are literally mountains of flesh and not one of them weighing less than 250-300 pounds? And how they fight with each other? Have you not wondered how wrestlers accomplish these seemingly superhuman feats without killing themselves or each other?

If someone hits you with a pulled punch that barely touches you, but you time it correctly and leap backward as though you had been smashed, it would appear real. How about the falls and slams? Wrestlers avoid injury by spreading out the force of impact; in judo they call it breakfall. No one ever gets slammed down directly onto his neck. Instead, they hit the mat back first.

Pro-wrestlers use specific methods to reduce pain and damage. One method involves maximizing the area of contact. Your elbow is hard and sharp. Your thigh, however, is larger and well padded by muscle and fat. If you jump from the top rope and land on someone, the damage inflicted by your elbow could literally kill them. If you did a leg drop and hit them with your outstretched thigh, the force would be spread out over a larger area. It would hurt and probably bruise, but it would not do nearly as much damage as an elbow.

In reality not a single match is ever real. The skills of the wrestlers do not determine the outcome of the match. Instead, writers work on plots and storylines well in advance, and every match is another chapter in the story. Who wins and who loses is all in the script. All the moves are choreographed. Wrestlers do not really try to beat up and injure the other but they merely act. They pretend as if they are greatly hurt, whereas in reality they are not. Most wrestlers are exceptional athletes who train for many hours each day to maintain their physical condition. They practice for years to learn both the moves and how to execute them safely while still making it look dangerous. They suffer many injuries, sometimes even severe.

Part X

TERRORISM

136

Can Terrorists Make LPG Or Petrol Tankers Explode Like Bombs By Shooting At Them?

This is a highly prevalent myth. People generally think that LPG tanker lorries or petrol tankers are bombs on wheels and that they would burst in a devastating explosion should a terrorist shoot at them or attach a small explosive charge to them. Sensational though it seems; it is not really possible.

To understand it properly, you must first understand how a flammable gas like LPG or petrol burns. The gas requires oxygen to burn. Have you ever thought why you require the gas burner at all? Could they have not simply attached a metal tube to the cylinder and you could have lighted at the other end? Would such a device work satisfactorily? No; because it would not be getting the required oxygen. For the LPG or petrol tanker to be converted into a bomb, all the fuel must burn simultaneously. This would require that all of the fuel be released in one go, allowed to mix with the proper amount of oxygen and then the mixture ignited simultaneously throughout its volume. The entire process must take place very rapidly as against accidents, which take quite some time to develop.

There are a lot of misconceptions regarding the bullet. You can shoot a bullet all right and it can rupture the skin of the tanker too. But it would not be able to deposit enough heat inside the tanker. The bullet is too small a thing and simply does not have enough heat in it. Hot gases propel it but the time of contact is too short for it to get any heat. You can rupture the cylinder with a bursting charge of high explosive. Still, the problem is that for a sudden rupture and release of the gas in a large volume, this desired mixing with oxygen does not take place efficiently. Then there is something called flash point below, which a fuel does not burn. A high explosive charge would generate heat at a point but would not be able to heat the fuel uniformly. Thus there is no risk of terrorists exploding tankers.

137

After Every Blast The Media Says That RDX Was Used: How Credible Are The Claims?

When following any terrorist bomb blast, the media instantly claims that RDX was used in the blast. In fact it would appear that no other explosive exists or that the terrorists would be excommunicated from the ranks of terrorists if they use any other explosive. RDX has caught the fancy of the media only recently. In the days of terrorism in Punjab, it was C-4 and Semtex. They have been forgotten now. How credible are these reports?

The reports are pure speculation. How? To understand this, you must understand how high explosives function and how they differ from low explosives. Gunpowder is an example of a low explosive. As we all know, it contains potassium nitrate, sulphur and charcoal. Sulphur and charcoal are the fuels while potassium nitrate is the oxidiser which provides oxygen for their burning. How then does the gunpowder explode? When you ignite it, it burns so fast that a large volume of hot gases is produced from the solids and these gases account for the explosion. The basic process is that of burning. A high explosive like dynamite, TNT or RDX does not burn. In them the large molecule of the explosive simply disintegrates into smaller gaseous molecules. There is no burning. This process is called detonation. It takes place several times faster than burning and that is why high explosives are more powerful.

When a low explosive explodes, chances are that the explosion of the part that burns first will scatter some of the mixture that is still not burnt. Thus at the scene of explosion a forensic analysis may find some explosive that is not burnt – it may be analysed in the laboratory to confirm the nature of the explosive. When a high explosive detonates, the process is so fast that no molecule remains undetonated. Hence it is extremely difficult to determine the nature of the explosive after the use of a high explosive. No inference can be drawn from the crater, etc. either. Thus the media reports are pure sensationalisations.

138

Can Terrorists Really Blow Up Dams?

One of the popular fantasies of the media is that terrorists may sneak into our dams and blow them up. Then there will be a deluge. All the water of the dam would gush forth and inundate large tracts of lands; killing may be millions of people.

Such an apprehension is based on pure ignorance. Actually people do not have an idea of the amount of explosives required for demolition of large structures. Most of the impressions are derived from films where even a grenade is shown bringing down a house or just a small block of explosive of the size of a school geometry box is shown bringing down a multi-storey building. Filmmakers can be pardoned for their stupidity. Actually explosives are not as powerful as they are generally made out to be. For demolition purposes, a great amount of explosives are required. A grenade has typically just about 100 grams of explosive. They can create splinters to kill humans but would not be enough to destroy even a heavy dining table.

Dams are massive structures in which thousands of tons of concrete is used. They are amongst the biggest man-made structures. The famous British scientist Sir Barnes Wallis had done research on that and found that even a medium size dam would require at least 30,000 pounds of high explosive to breach it. When very carefully deployed at the correct depth, it could be brought down to 10,000 pounds but not less. His famous dam buster bombs, which breached dams like Mohne and Eder in Germany in the Second World War, were of 10,000 pounds. Now which terrorist group in the world can manage 10,000 pounds of explosive in one place? And even if they can, how will they carry it? They do not have bomber aircrafts! Even armies do not have so much explosive in one place. Hence the fear of terrorists destroying dams is baseless. Dams are so strong that even a few hundred pounds of explosive would not even scratch them.

139

Can Terrorists Really Unleash Biological Warfare On Huge Populations?

Following the 9/11 attacks, the western world has been gripped by paranoia that the terrorists may unleash biological warfare on them. You may recall, how afraid they were of anthrax and how buildings got vacated if someone found even talcum powder in some paper! Since Indian media copies everything from the West, they have copied this fear also. People are afraid that the terrorists may spread strange diseases in India.

Such apprehensions are based on pure ignorance. Most people have no idea as to how biological agents can be used as warfare and how complex the process is. It is not that you simply take the sputum of a cow suffering from anthrax and mix it in the town water supply for everyone to get anthrax. Since the modern man has immunity against a large number of diseases and there are easily available medicines for most diseases, first one must develop or isolate the right strain of the organism for which the target people would not have immunity or which is a more virulent strain of some existing pathogen. One may have to genetically modify some strains. You should have them in spore form for storage with spores of just the right size. Finally you need a dependable release or delivery mechanism. You cannot wage biological war by sending spores in an envelope or spraying them from a single-seat aircraft.

The specific technologies used in realizing these capabilities are very complex and include cell culture or fermentation; organism selection; encapsulation and coating with straight or cross-linked biopolymers; genetic engineering; active or passive immunisation or treatment with biological response modifiers; monoclonal antibody production; genome databases, polymerase chain reaction equipment, DNA sequencers and the rapid production of gene probes; and the capability of linking gene probes and monoclonal antibodies on addressable sites in a reproducible manner. These are beyond the capability of most nations, and far more impossible for terrorist groups.

140

Can Terrorists Resort To Chemical Warfare Or Use Chemical Agents In Their Attacks?

Quite often we hear rumours that terrorists could poison water supply tanks and thousands of people would die. Next to biological warfare, this is the biggest fear of the western world. After all, the USA went to war against Saddam Hussain alleging that he had been building chemical warfare weapons. It is a different thing that nothing was ever found.

There are several types of chemical agents that can be used in warfare. Terrorists can only make the simplest ones because making the advanced ones requires knowledge and technologies, which are just not available with terrorist groups. Simple agents include chlorine, phosgene and mustard gas. Making nerve agents like Tabun, Soman, Sarin and VX, VG, etc. is very difficult. Anyone who thinks that a person with a Masters in chemistry can make them is sadly mistaken – he is not likely to know even their formula, not to speak of the method of preparation.

There is another serious problem in using chemical agents. Merely making the chemical is not enough, you have to disseminate it effectively in the target area and that is a major technical challenge. You also require considerable quantities of the agent. It is not that you find out the formula after some research and then proceed to produce some in your backyard. Even if you do, the quantity produced will be very little. When chemical agents are released in open atmosphere, they disperse quickly and that increases the amount of chemical required. Unless a terrorist is using them in a closed space, he is not likely to have enough quantity for any effective use. Then the problem is how to disperse. When the USA developed chemical agents, they designed them to be delivered by aircrafts or by artillery shells whereas terrorists do not have them. Shells are good only for an area which is the size of a badminton court and aircrafts needed tonnes of chemicals.

Terrorists can at most poison wells or small tanks of a colony or so. Municipal tanks are so huge that the quantity of poison used for a well would simply be lost in them.

141

Can Terrorists Make And Use The So-Called 'Dirty Nuclear Bombs'?

One of the common fears of the media is the so-called 'dirty nuclear bomb'. What is a dirty nuclear bomb? How did they come into existence? You see the media has realised that it would be difficult for the terrorists to make proper nuclear bombs as the technical sophistication and the resources required are way beyond their capability. However, if the media let go of something sensational then what they would publish in the papers or show on the TV channels. Thus the dirty bomb was born. It has been given a technical name also – radiological dispersal device. The fear is that terrorists could spread radioactive material in the air with the help of conventional explosives. Is it possible? Not really.

If someone could get suitable radioactive material in sufficient quantities, he can easily make one. But please note 'suitable' and 'sufficient'. The radioactive material should have a reasonably high level of radioactivity and the half-life should not be too short (half-life is the time in which radioactivity becomes half of the starting value). It should also lend itself to easy dispersal in the form of a very fine dust; they have to be pulverised to micron-size particles and mixed with something that could increase the chances of inhalation. Then it should be in sufficient quantities for dispersal over a fairly large area to make sense as a weapon. Remember that in a built-up area the dispersal would be poor and in an open area one requires suitable weather conditions. When all these requirements are taken together, making one does not appear to be very difficult. But from where will they get such materials? Pilfering from the radioactive sources used in radiotherapy and in industry is not going to help much as the quantities used are very small; it would not make even one man sick. The best they can do is to go for radioactive waste from commercial nuclear reactors. But that is very carefully guarded and monitored. Nowhere in the world there has been a single instance of radioactive waste being lost or looted from nuclear reactor sites.

Part XI

MYTHS PROPAGATED BY FILMS

142

Will The Earth Be Destroyed If It Is Hit By An Asteroid Or Comet?

For long mankind has been afraid that if a sufficiently large asteroid hits the earth, the earth would be destroyed. They say that the impact could kick up so much dust in the atmosphere that it would block the rays of the sun and that would be bad for life. One of the theories advanced for the extinction of the dinosaurs is that such an impact ushered in the Ice Age; they were not able to adopt and therefore died.

The fact is that all such theories are essentially conjectures. This is a hundreds of millions of year old planet and something could have hit the earth in such a long period. Every day, thousands of meteors fall on the earth – most of them get burnt in the sky. Only the large ones reach the surface. Some scientists have claimed that they have found evidence of such a hit 251 million years ago by a six mile wide asteroid. They analysed some rocky fragments recovered on a place called Graphite Peak in Antarctica. They say that the chemical composition of the rocks is almost the same as that found in meteorites. Hence they conclude that those must be the fragments of the asteroid that hit there. Similar rocks were found in China also; they say that the fragments must have been fallen that far. It sounds quite exciting.

But other scientists like Jeffrey Grossman of the US Geological Survey have raised more fundamental doubts. They say that it is extremely unlikely that something like meteorite rocks could have remained chemically unchanged over 251 million years. You leave anything anywhere and the atmosphere affects it and 251 million years is a very long time.

This is an example of how even scientists get influenced by popular writings. Dan Brown imagined exactly this sort of thing in his novel *Deception Point*. The scientists had read that and it hung at the back of their minds. When they did their research, they tried to fit in their findings to their preconceived notions.

143

Can We Save The Earth From An Asteroid Hurtling Towards Us By Blowing It Up Using A Hydrogen Bomb?

Americans love heroics. In the process they create myths and legends that linger for a long time. There is a Bruce Willis film called Armageddon in which an asteroid is all set to hit the earth in 18 days. Smaller fragments have already destroyed parts of New York and Paris and 50,000 people have died in Shanghai. The Americans fly to the asteroid, drill an 800 feet hole, plant a hydrogen bomb in it and blow it up in two parts which fly past the earth. The leader Bruce Willis heroically gives up his life to save humanity as he stays behind to activate the bomb.

Unfortunately it cannot be done in practice. Do not think that you can explode a hydrogen bomb close to the asteroid and it will be blown to bits. When a bomb is exploded in the air, water or ground, much of the damage by the blast is caused by the sudden heating of the surrounding matter to millions of degrees, which produces the explosive force. When you explode a bomb in the vacuum of space there is nothing to get heated up. If you have to do something, you will have to drill a hole in the asteroid and plant a bomb deep into its bowels, quite like what Bruce Willis did.

But that is not practical. In the first place, we do not have the technology at present to shoot a missile precisely into an asteroid millions of miles away, so forget about landing a rocket there and the heroic crew drilling a hole into the solid rock for the bomb to be planted. The drilling equipment is extremely heavy and big. Where do you have rockets that can carry such huge and heavy equipment? Above all, we do not have such big hydrogen bombs which will destroy an asteroid nearly ten miles wide. We could perhaps hope that an explosion near the surface of the asteroid could perhaps change its orbit somewhat so that it could miss the earth.

144

Do Grenades Produce A Ball Of Fire When They Explode And Can They Throw Men Around?

This is a familiar shot in films. The hero pulls the pin out of the grenade using his teeth and throws the grenade, which produces a large ball of fire, and men are thrown up in air. Grenades are not designed to produce fireballs in the first place. Most of the grenades are anti-personnel grenades that are designed to kill or injure people. For this they must produce fragments. Fragmented grenades contain a small explosive charge in a metal or polymer body, designed to break into fragments when the charge explodes. The explosive charge is just about 5–6.5 ounces.

When the explosive charge of TNT or Composition B explodes, it does not produce a fireball. High explosives like TNT are materially different from low explosives like gunpowder used in firecrackers. When you explode a firecracker, the powder burns. It is the burning which produces the flash and the smoke. High explosives do not burn but when they explode, their molecules break into gaseous molecules. Hence there is no question of a fireball.

The only grenades that produce fire are incendiary grenades. They have an incendiary composition, which actually burns and are used to start fire but they cannot be used as anti-personnel grenades as shown in the films. In films the grenade is merely thrown. The photo of explosion is not that of the grenade at all. They use simple petrol or gelled petrol to produce the fireball. The fuel is burnt using a small bursting charge that produces the fireball.

The films also show men flying as a result of the explosion. That is also pure myth – grenade has so little explosive that there is no question of throwing a man around. They can kill men by fragments but the total explosive force produced is very little. The shrapnel of a grenade are like bullets. The explosive force of the cartridge of a pistol gives only recoil to the hand. It does not make you fly. Similarly, a grenade cannot make you fly.

145

Can Locks Be Broken By Shooting At Them With Pistols Or Revolvers?

This is a staple of films, both Hollywood and Bollywood. The hero encounters a locked door; he whips out his pistol and shoots the padlock. Can this work in real life?

No. Pistol and revolver bullets are not hard objects. Bullets are made of lead which is a soft metal; in fact so soft that you can scratch it with your nails. Why are bullets made of lead? Because the density of lead is much higher than that of iron and a denser metal means that a bullet of the same size will be heavier. A heavier bullet will be more stable in flight. Secondly, bullets are supposed to injure humans. For that, it is better to have a soft bullet. Soft bullets get deformed on hitting bones and then create a worse wound. In fact bullets with a very soft nose, would spread like a mushroom upon impact (called Dum-Dum bullets), have been banned since decades. Such bullets are not designed to damage steel or brass sheets as you would find in padlocks. They are designed to damage flesh.

Scientists shot at padlocks using the standard 9 mm pistol and even .357 magnum revolvers but they could not break the locks. There is no chance at all if you shoot at the shackle of the lock. Shackles are made of very hard steel, which is too hard for the bullet to do anything and it is cylindrical in cross-section. Chances are that the bullet will simply ricochet and hit something unintended. Even if you shoot at the body of the lock or the plates, the bullet would be deformed in the process and would not be able to break critical components of the lock. They may damage some parts of the lock but the whole thing would still hold.

A lock can be broken with LG or SSG shots of a 12 bore shotgun, which would fire about 10-15 large size pellets at the lock and together they will inflict sufficient damage on the lock for it to break.

146

Do Cars Really Fly Up In The Air If The Fuel Tank Explodes Or When They Run Over A Landmine?

One of the most exciting shots of films are those where cars fly in the air as a result of a bomb exploding inside, or their fuel tanks exploding or their having run over a landmine.

Suppose a bomb explodes inside a car. This means that the explosive force of the bomb is applied in all the directions. It can rip apart a car but there is no net force in any single direction if the bomb is centrally placed. There may be a slight imbalance of forces depending upon where the bomb explodes inside the car but there is no way the imbalance could be so great as to lift the car up bodily. The same argument applies to an exploding fuel tank.

The case of a car running over a landmine is based upon a different misconception. Real landmines have high explosives like Composition B. High explosives produce a shattering effect. It is only low explosives that propel. For example, the propellant in a cartridge is a low explosive. It propels the bullet. If you fill the cartridge with high explosive, the gun would burst. Landmines are designed to shatter the bottoms of vehicles so that either the vehicle is disabled or the occupants killed by shrapnel or both. They are not intended to lift the vehicle up in the air as that would not serve any purpose.

Then, how do they make the cars fly in the air as they show in the films? If the car needs to flip or jump, a large pneumatic air ram is bolted into the car. If the ram points down, it can be triggered by the driver to fire a pole at the ground, propelling the car into a flip. An air ram pointing backward can launch a car into an impressive jump. If men are to be shown flying then they are propelled by air rams, spring-loaded platforms and trampolines or pulled by a wire system. The explosions are added in the shot just for the visual effect.

147

How Do People Jump Through Glasses In Films?

Hollywood or Bollywood, it is a common sight in films. The hero jumps through glasses to enter a room where the heroine is in a serious danger of getting killed or raped, or at other times villains get thrown out of windows after they receive some solid punch or kick. And yet no one gets injured at the end of the day – not even a scratch! Then you also find people breaking bottles on the heads of the other. If you do such things in real life, it might result in serious injuries or even death. Then how do they do it in films?

Scientists have done experiments on this. It has been found that while it is possible to crash through a ⅛ inch glass pane with little or no injuries, ¼ inch glass is thick enough to inflict significant lacerations on a body, should one be thrown through it. In film stunts, a breakaway faux-glass substance called sugar glass is used for stunts requiring an actor to be thrown through a window. Sugar glass does not break into sharp fragments like real glass does and nor does it injure stunt performers.

Sugar glass (also called candy glass) is not glass at all, but a mixture of sugar, corn syrup and water, which looks like glass when finished. How do they make sugar glass? The recipe is simple. Take two cups of water, one cup of white corn syrup, three-and-a-half cups of sugar and ¼ tsp of creamy tartar. Mix the water, corn syrup, sugar and tartar together in a pot and bring it to a boil on the stove (at about 220°F). Leave it for boiling till it reaches 300°F, which will take about 45 minutes. The mixture should be thick, with most of the water being evaporated. As soon as it hits 300°F, pour it into whatever mould you are using and let it cool.

Once the sugar glass has been made, it must be used immediately. Otherwise, it will warp and become soft and sticky. Hence for films it is made just before its use in a shot.

148

How Do They Show A Burning Man In Films?

This stunt has been the staple of films across the world. What could be more spectacular than a man on fire? How do they do it? Can stuntmen really risk their lives by setting fire to their bodies? In some of the films they simply cheat, particularly in scenes where someone on fire is shown jumping or pushed from a high building or cliff and where they can afford a long shot – then they simply use dummies.

However, in good quality cinema many of the scenes are not camera tricks. Though professional stuntmen are used as doubles, scenes in which someone is actually set on fire are among the most dangerous ever filmed. How is it done? The first thing to do is protect the person's body. You cannot show a naked person set on fire.

The stuntman actually wears several layers of protective clothing, including fire-resistant materials like asbestos inside. Special gloves and a hood cover the hands and head. In most burn scenes, the hood is clearly evident, though its appearance can be minimised by good editing. Inside the hood is a small breathing apparatus connected to a small oxygen tank so that the man is not killed due to lack of air. The performer is then coated in a specially prepared flammable gel. This is the most important part. They are not simply doused in petrol as they show because that would be suicidal. Petrol is too inflammable to be used in stunts. The specially prepared gel is not so inflammable and burns slowly that it can be doused quickly. The liquid they pour on the body is not at all inflammable. It is only for dramatic effect. Before the gel is lit, multiple extinguishers and paramedics must be ready at the scene. The burn itself is carefully timed and the amount of gel used is carefully calculated.

The burn scene shown in the films has to be for a short period of time. It cannot be made too long, otherwise it will prove fatal.

149

Does A Man Hit By A Bullet Fall Backwards?

This kind of incident has occurred end number of times in films. A man is hit by a bullet and he falls backwards as if he has been pushed hard by some invisible hand. In some films you may even see people flying backwards and toppling over railings. Is it possible?

The answer is a categorical no. The law of conservation of momentum states that the total momentum of a collection of various objects that are interacting with each other in some way remains constant. Now momentum is nothing but mass multiplied by velocity. Velocity is speed with a direction. When a man is holding the pistol in his hand – he, the pistol and the bullet are at rest. It means the total momentum of the system is zero and come what may, the total momentum of the system of the shooter, the pistol and the bullet will remain zero. When the bullet is fired, it rushes forward with a certain momentum. This means that in order to keep the total momentum zero, the shooter and the pistol must move backwards with the same momentum. This is what you feel as the recoil of the firing. Now since the man is much heavier than the bullet, his velocity is very low and the person towards whom the bullet is shot gets a jerk, that is all. The momentum of a small bullet flying at a high speed is equal to the momentum that the jerk produced in a much heavier man.

Now if you are firing a bullet and it strikes a man, i.e. the bullet is lodged in his body, this means that the bullet after striking the man comes to rest. Thus all the momentum of the bullet is transferred to the man struck. We just saw that the bullet has only as much momentum which is enough to give a man a little jerk. This cannot throw a man backwards or make him topple over a railing. If the bullet were to have as much momentum, even the shooter would be thrown backwards!

150

Gunshots And Gunshot Wounds: How Are They Made In Films?

Can there be an action film without guns? Guns are integral to films. Never mind that the guns used in films seem to have an inexhaustible supply of ammunition in their magazines. Revolvers fire scores of rounds and the bullets get exhausted only when the story demands it.

Are the guns and bullets for real? Mostly not. The guns may be real at times but live ammunition is never used on a film site. Guns are either extremely well-made fakes, or loaded with blanks or ammunition that makes a loud noise and produces a flame too but does not shoot a bullet. It should be noted that blanks can fire compressed gases or bits of metal or cardboard, so they are still dangerous to the face and eyes, especially at a close range. These days fake guns are made so well that they look as good as real.

The impression of the impact of a bullet on a human body is produced by using squibs. A squib is a small explosive charge (today a pneumatic charge is often used) taped to the victim's body in the appropriate place, with a small bag of fake blood on top of it. The whole rig is backed with a metal plate, protecting the actor from the charge and projecting it outward. The charges are set off remotely, or by the actor himself, via a button hidden in his sleeve, timed to the firing of a gun in the scene. When the charges go off, it rips through clothing and spurts the fake blood in a convincing facsimile image of a gunshot wound. If the squibs are not well made you can actually see a small explosion at the point where the real bullet enters.

Scenes of bullet hitting on other surfaces are filmed by drilling proper holes, covering them with painted putty or paper, then setting off charges to blow away the cover and reveal the hole.